# Policy and Practice in Bibliographic Control of Nonbook Media

Edited by
Sheila S. Intner
and
Richard P. Smiraglia

for the Resources and
Technical Services Division,
American Library Association

American Library Association
Chicago and London 1987

Cover designed by Ellen Pettengell

Text designed by Ray Machura

Composed by Graphic World, Inc. in
Linotron Melior and Univers

Printed on 50-pound Glatfelter, a
pH-neutral stock, and bound in
10-point Carolina cover stock by
Cushing-Malloy, Inc.

**Library of Congress Cataloging-in-Publication Data**

Policy and practice in bibliographic control of nonbook media.

    1.  Libraries—Special collections—Non-book materials.
2.  Audio-visual library service.  3.  Cataloging of nonbook materials.  I.  Intner, Sheila S.  II.  Smiraglia,
Richard P.  III.  American Library Association. Resources
and Technical Services Division.
Z688.N6P65  1987      025.3'4      87-1849
ISBN: 0-8389-0468-8

◻

◻ Contents

# ☐ Foreword

One of the fastest growing areas in librarianship is the acquisition and organization of nonbook materials. No longer just the task of school libraries, today every type of library must collect nonbook materials in its pursuit of access to information for its clientele.

The ability to interface video technology, computer technology, and the new sound technologies of compact laser discs have presented many challenges to librarians. Just as librarians master a new technology, another comes onto the scene. Rarely do any of the new technologies supplant the older ones; libraries do not throw out older media just because a new form has been developed. All of these materials must be organized in a way that will provide easy access to the information they contain.

In 1978, when *Anglo-American Cataloguing Rules*, second edition, was published, some of the formats that now must be cataloged were not viewed as meaningful parts of a library's collection. Who could foresee then that by 1986 machine-readable data files or microcomputer software would be integral parts of library collections in all types of libraries? Rules in *AACR2* have had to be interpreted, and in some instances revised, to accommodate the integration of these new technologies into the library's catalog in a meaningful manner.

For too long nonprint materials have been outside the mainstream of a library's collection. Both the acquisition and the organization of nonprint materials have been separate operations. Now in the mid-1980s we are beginning to see a change. In states such as New Jersey and Illinois, there is a movement to include nonprint materials in library networks and cooperation as has been done with print materials for years. Not only is cataloging copy being shared but also the materials themselves. The fear that nonprint materials will be damaged through interlibrary loan is slowly on the wane. In New Jersey, for example, when needs assessments were taken in several regions, the availability of nonprint materials through interlibrary loan was given a higher priority than print materials.

Nonbook materials are growing in numbers. Their availability in all types of libraries has caused major concern on how to integrate this material into collections. A particular concern is how to provide access to their varied artistic and intellectual content. This book, which is an outgrowth of a series of regional institutes on nonbook materials, sponsored by the Resources and Technical Services Division, looks at nonbook materials from historical and current perspectives. It covers acquisition and collection development of nonbook materials, access to information, and the cataloging of special formats of nonbook materials.

Information comes in many formats, all of which must be organized into an integrated whole with ease of access for patrons to the intellectual content. The integration of nonbook materials into collections will challenge libraries as we move toward the twenty-first century.

WILLIAM I. BUNNELL
Executive Director
Resources and Technical Services Division
American Library Association

☐
☐ Editors' Introduction

This book is based on the regional institutes on nonbook materials sponsored by the Resources and Technical Services Division (RTSD) of the American Library Association and the RTSD Council on Regional Groups. The idea for an RTSD-sponsored road show devoted to nonbook materials was the brainchild of Nancy B. Olson. It grew out of a workshop on the cataloging of nonbook materials that she led during the Annual Conference of the American Library Association in Los Angeles in 1981. Richard P. Smiraglia led the second half of that workshop, covering printed music and musical sound recordings. Several other members of the institute's faculty participated in the workshop as leaders of small group discussions.

The objectives (as stated in their brochures) of the regional institutes on nonbook materials were:

1. to gain an understanding of the process of acquisitions, organizations, and access to nonbook materials
2. to learn about standards for bibliographic control for nonbook materials, emphasizing microcomputer software . . . state-of-the-art audio and video technologies, and all other nonbook media
3. to gain an insight into the impact of cooperative networking and computerization in relation to nonbook materials
4. to explore the future of nonbook materials in libraries
5. to demonstrate microcomputer applications for library technical services

The institutes were designed to reach librarians with responsibility for acquisitions and cataloging of nonbook materials in all types of libraries, library educators, and media center administrators.

A particular concern of the institutes' planning faculty was to reach public and school librarians. Over a two-year period, institutes were held in San Diego, Washington, Chicago, Orlando, and Boston. Despite heroic efforts to keep costs at a minimum, the total package for a weekend institute was beyond the reach of many librarians from institutions anxious to improve their treatment of nonbook collections. Thus, the faculty decided to translate their oral presentations into a book in hopes of reaching the audience they originally set out to address.

The chapters in Part 1 of this book were originally given as speeches during the institute's plenary sessions. Jean Weihs set the stage for each institute, as she does here, by setting forth an historical context in which to understand nonbook materials. After the first institute, the faculty realized that a clear delineation of the theoretical principles on which all organization of materials rested was missing from its agenda. Richard P. Smiraglia supplied the missing link, and his "Bibliographic Control Theory and Nonbook Materials" is an easily read scholarly exposition of these principles.

Sheila S. Intner's "Developing Nonbook Collections" and Hugh A. Durbin's "Using Policy Statements to Define and Manage the Nonbook Collection" also address umbrella topics—general problems of amassing and administering the nonbook collections for which specific control processes are discussed later on. Networking, a progressively more important method of obtaining library materials for users, is discussed by Lizbeth Bishoff in "Cooperation and Networking."

Jean Weihs addresses overall issues of subject access in "Access to Nonbook Materials: The Role of Subject Headings and Classification Numbers. . . ." These thorny problems are often overlooked in the more frenetic search for adequate descriptive cataloging for nonbook materials.

Equally critical in the maintenance of an effective catalog is authority control, explained thoroughly by Arlene G. Taylor in "Authority Control and System Design." Taylor, though not a member of the institute faculty, was invited by them to contribute this chapter. It covers this important subject extremely well and is based on original research. It is applicable to both book and nonbook materials in its analysis of the structures of authority control.

Carolyn O. Frost also was invited to contribute her chapter, "Nonbook Materials in the Online Public Access Catalog." This thorough review of the state of the art of that subject outlines current and future possibilities for access to nonbook materials through implementation of computer-based catalogs. Increasingly, librarians are turning to computer-based systems to furnish the services and information traditionally unavailable from card and/ or book catalogs that people trying to access nonbook materials desperately need.

Part 1 closes with Leigh S. Estabrook's "Current and Future Needs of the Catalog: A User's Perspective," an hilarious account of user befuddlement in trying to locate desired nonbook materials. Estabrook asks searching questions and gives us clues to their answers, though librarians have yet to find them.

Adaptations of cataloging workshops for specific media make up Part 2. These six chapters of the book cover the cataloging of music scores and sound recordings (by Richard P. Smiraglia), motion pictures and videorecordings (by Sheila S. Intner), two- and three-dimensional materials (by Lizbeth Bishoff), microcomputer software (by Nancy B. Olson), and the coding and tagging of bibliographic data for nonbook materials for MARC format entry (by Sheila S. Intner). Among the faculty teaching them, the first workshop was known as "Sound and Music," the one on two- and three-dimensional materials was called "Toys and Games," and the tagging and coding workshop was known as "Funny Fields."

Some of the basic issues which are discussed in both parts of this work include:

1. integrating bibliographic data for nonbook materials in library catalogs
2. intershelving nonbook materials with books
3. integrating management processes, including budgeting, staffing, and collection management
4. librarians' attitudes toward nonbook materials
5. adherence to standards
6. innovative thinking concerning nonbook materials.

These issues will be recognized as basic to library organization and administration and may be taken for granted with regard to book collections. For nonbook collections, however, they are still hotly debated.

The whole point of this book, and the entire effort to bring the institutes on nonbook materials to audiences throughout the United States, is that information—that precious resource—occurs in a variety of forms, each of which is important to the library's public. This is true whether we speak of public libraries, libraries in colleges and universities, primary and secondary school libraries, or libraries in corporations, research institutions, or other special environments. The free flow of information from creator to consumer is the chief goal of library and information service. Libraries can achieve this goal through collection and dissemination of resources—nonbook as well as book.

It is our hope that this book will contribute to enhanced use of nonbook materials in all library settings.

Part

# 1

# Background, Theory, and Management Concerns

# ■ A Taste of Nonbook History: Historical Background and Review of the State of the Art of Bibliographic Control of Nonbook Materials

by Jean Weihs

*Though efforts to standardize the bibliographic control of nonbook materials in libraries have gained steam only in recent times, libraries have been collecting and circulating nonbook materials for many years. Jean Weihs, currently the chair of the Joint Steering Committee for the Revision of the Anglo-American Cataloguing Rules, has been at the forefront of developments in standardized bibliographic control of nonbook materials for nearly two decades. Here she renders a scholarly account of the forces that combined to bring these developments to a head in AACR2, thus providing an historical context in which to understand the state of the art in bibliographic control of nonbook materials.*

*Beginning with an account of the earliest major collections of maps at the British Museum Library and the Library of Congress in 1801, Weihs traces milestones such as the first public circulation of nonbook materials in the mid-nineteenth century and the phenomenal growth in production and use of nonbook materials in the second half of this century. Though problems in systematic cataloging of nonbook materials were recognized as early as the 1920s, true efforts at standardization began only in the late 1950s. Weihs provides a detailed account of the development of the landmark Nonbook Materials: The Organization of Integrated Collections, on which developments culminating in the simultaneous production of AACR2 and ISBD (NBM) were based.*

Covering nonbook cataloging, its past history, present status, and future possibilities in the space of a chapter is a difficult task. The many boxes of source documents in my basement attest to the fact

Jean Weihs is Course Director in Library Techniques at Seneca College of Applied Arts and Technology, Ontario, Canada, and author of *Nonbook Materials: The Organization of Integrated Collections* and *Accessible Storage of Nonbook Materials*.

that I have participated in some of the history since 1967, yet when I read accounts or chronologies of those years, I find important events missing or contradictory statements made. For example, in one article by a Library of Congress staff member, two different dates are given for the beginning of printing cards for motion pictures. Tracking history is a frustrating job for someone with limited time for research.

Where does one start researching the advent of nonbook materials in libraries? Surely, there were maps in the great library of Alexandria and in many medieval libraries. The realization has come slowly that an authoritative history could fill volumes. Not wanting to usurp the entire book, I offer the following therefore as just a taste of nonbook history.

## The Early Years of Collecting

Was it coincidence that the Library of Congress (LC) and the British Museum acquired maps about the same time? Charles Goodrum in his book *The Library of Congress* states that shortly after LC was founded the initial order of books received from London included ". . . a special case tightly packed with maps."[1] When the Ordnance Survey in Great Britain started to publish maps in 1801, a copy of each was deposited with the British Museum. Did the order sent to London by LC in June 1800 arrive at the LC before the British Museum collection started? Did LC "win by a nose" the honor of having the earlier map collection? It would be fun to find the answer. However, the important point is that nonbook materials have had a place in library collections for a long time.

The earliest date I found in connection with nonbook materials organized for public circulation was 1889. In this year the Denver Public Library organized its picture collection for use by its clients. By 1897 LC had pictures and photographs. Sound archives were found in Vienna in 1899. There appear to have been sound recordings in U.S. libraries around the turn of the century, but exact dates and places are difficult to pinpoint. The year 1913 is mentioned as the time a sound collection was established in St. Paul, Minnesota. National archives for film and sound recordings were established in both the United States and Great Britain in 1935; in that same year there is evidence of a motion picture collection at the Museum of Modern Art (New York), although it did not become part of the general collection until after World War II.

By 1940 approximately 25 public libraries and several university libraries in the United States had nonbook collections; only two public libraries and no university libraries in Great Britain had nonbook collections available to the public. Europe, however, had none, since nonbook materials came to European public libraries in the 1950s.

Since the mid-1950s there has been an enormous growth in the number and size of collections. For example, in 1950 nonbook materials were less than 10 percent of LC's holdings; by 1980 nonbook materials were more than 20 percent of this collection. Therefore, because of LC's prominent position as a collector of materials and administrator of copyright, we can assume that production of nonbook materials increased at a faster rate than that of book materials during these years. This is one reason many librarians became aware of these materials in the 1960s. A mass market for such materials and their broad commercial distribution developed in these years.

The increase in nonbook materials in libraries—particularly school libraries—was largely due to the rise in government financing of educational programs both in the United States and Canada. I well remember that in the Province of Ontario, where I work, money for educational purposes seemed limitless in the 1960s. This was the golden age of educational experimentation and innovation. This was also the decade when the disadvantaged child was "discovered." Educators were looking for materials designed to reach this type of child, who seemed to respond to nonbook materials more effectively than to books. Prompted by this influx of money and these educational needs, publishers and manufacturers flooded the market with a plethora of nonbook titles and formats.

Before the 1960s most nonbook collections were single-medium collections, frequently housed away from the books which remained the base stock of a library's resources. The public, and many times the staff as well, were not aware of the existence of these collections. As the wealth of nonbook resources became apparent to staff members, a desire to integrate them into the general collection grew. Of course, if they were to be part of the general collection, they had to be cataloged.

When did libraries start to catalog their nonbook collections in a systematic way? The answer to this question is elusive; I found intriguing, though sometimes conflicting, information. For instance, Arundell Esdaile, in his book *The British Museum Li-*

brary, states that the British Museum started cataloging maps in 1841,[2] but the 1906 edition of the British Museum cataloging rules is the first time rules for map cataloging were given.

In a book published in 1922, Dorcas Fellows recognized problems that sound familiar today:

> ... if with the entries for books there could be included entries for illustrative objects also it would undoubtedly add greatly to the use of ... available resources, both books and illustrative objects.[3]

The introduction to *Rules for Descriptive Cataloging in the Library of Congress: Phonorecords* states:

> ... systematic cataloging of sound recordings began at least 15 years ago in the music divisions of some of the larger public and university libraries.[4]

The book was published in 1952, and simple arithmetic produces the date 1937 as the beginning of systematic cataloging for sound recordings.

Before 1950 there were only a few guides and articles on the subject. The first approaches were developed in response to the needs of particular libraries. As centralized cataloging became more common, the need for standards emerged. Because of their rapidly developing nonbook collections, school libraries developed standards at the district level and eventually at the state level. However, each group worked in isolation, producing rules that did not match those developed elsewhere. Commercial catalogers were reluctant to adopt any particular standard, so they developed their own rules. The result was bibliographic chaos.

One aspect of this chaos was the difficulty of identifying materials for interlibrary loan. Each set of rules had different criteria for the source of the title, which made the correct identification of a particular item a game of chance.

The first detailed analysis of nonbook cataloging was done at the Library of Congress, and rules were published between 1952 and 1965 covering motion pictures, filmstrips, sound recordings, and two-dimensional representations. These rules, designed for use at LC for single-medium catalogs, were approved as the official rules for the U.S. cataloging community by the American Library Association.

An important meeting was held in Norman, Oklahoma, in 1969. Pearce Grove organized Systems and Standards for Bibliographic Control of Media, a three-week institute that brought together 49 participants from three countries—the United States, Canada, and Great Britain. It was an opportunity for these participants, who were all involved in searching for effective bibliographic control, to exchange views and to understand the state of the art in other parts of the world. In the long term this institute made a contribution to the easy exchange of information among the participants and to the eventual agreement on international standards.

I have mentioned that the 1960s was the decade of the amalgamation of nonbook materials with the general collection. It was also a time when librarians began to see the advantages of having all records for a collection in a single catalog, referred to as *integrated* or *omnimedia* catalogs. The *Anglo-American Cataloging Rules (AACR)* was published in 1967. Part III, which dealt with nonbook materials, was a disappointment to many librarians who wanted to produce omnimedia catalogs because it was based on the LC rules previously noted. *AACR* dealt with each medium separately without regard for integration. For example, the rules for entry and description differed from medium to medium. If a Picasso painting was reproduced on a poster, the poster was entered under the name of the artist and was not given a medium designation; if the same painting was reproduced as a slide, the slide was entered under title and had a medium designation. These rules made an integrated catalog a difficult proposition. In addition, *AACR* did not cover all the media found in library collections. As a result, Part III was used by few librarians.

## Experiences in the 1960s

I first became aware of nonbook materials in libraries in 1967, having to grapple with their cataloging. I thought this lack of awareness was because of my career path, that I had happened to work in libraries which had few nonbook materials in their collections. However, I have since learned that other librarians also became aware of these materials in the 1960s. Thus, my story, up to a point, is a universal example of a cataloger's experience in those years.

I was faced with cataloging the nonbook materials in the school libraries of a borough of metropolitan Toronto. As a librarian I firmly believe that if you can read, you can do anything. However, I found little to read on the subject, and that little gave me contradictory instructions. I then called people whom I knew had nonbook collections and asked their opinions. They described their cataloging procedures and each one ended by saying, "Don't do what I did; it doesn't work very well." After considerable investigation, I had nothing. I then contacted Shirley Lewis and Janet Macdonald, who were at that time heads of the cataloging departments of local commercial catalogers, and suggested that we decide on what rules we were going to use in the city of Toronto, so that at least in that area we would be consistent and would be able to conduct interlibrary loans. We started a small committee to work on the rules.

To this point our experience was typical. From here on it becomes astonishing. Within three months I received calls from many parts of the North American continent asking about our work and inviting either me or the three of us to come to talk about nonbook cataloging. In one year I was on 39 flights. It is obvious that we were investigating a very pressing problem at the right moment.

During our travels we met members of the Department of Audio-Visual Instruction (DAVI—a part of the National Education Association in the United States), now called the Association for Educational Communications and Technology (AECT). They were also working on a manual. However, at that time they had no interest in books or in multimedia collections. This attitude changed in later years.

The end result of our investigations was the conclusion that all materials in a library should be cataloged according to rules based on the same cataloging concepts, and, since most libraries would be unwilling to recatalog their book collections, the rules for nonbook materials had to fit the concepts for books found in Parts I and II of *AACR*.

The preliminary edition of *Nonbook Materials: The Organization of Integrated Collections*, published in 1970 by the Canadian Library Association,[5] was written for libraries which wished to have a multimedia catalog. Therefore, its rules followed the rules for books as much as possible. *Nonbook Materials* was recommended by the Canadian Library Association Council and by the American Library Association, Resources and Technical Services Division, Cataloging and Classification Section Executive Committee ". . . as an interim guide for the cataloging of nonbook materials, with the proviso that a permanent ALA/CLA committee be established to work on any necessary revisions for the final edition and its supplements."[6] It was also officially adopted in Australia and unofficially in two South American countries. We invited comments on the book's contents and to our surprise received about 250 letters, telephone calls, and personal communications from North America, Great Britain and the European continent, South America, and Saudi Arabia.

## Developments in the Seventies

The first edition of *Nonbook Materials: The Organization of Integrated Collections* was published in 1973 in consultation with the Joint Advisory Committee on Nonbook Materials, representing four American and Canadian national professional organizations. We examined all the comments sent to us as a result of the preliminary edition and included those which were pertinent. An innovation in this edition was the idea of entry under performer. The committee representatives had asked us to do this as a trial run. It was a successful experiment, and this idea was later incorporated into *AACR2*.

The transition from *AACR* to *AACR2* was eased for nonbook materials by the publication in 1975 and 1976 of a revised and expanded version of Chapter 12 (Special Audiovisual Materials) and a revised Chapter 14 (Sound Recordings).[7]

The *International Standard Bibliographic Description: Nonbook Materials*, or ISBD (NBM), was published in 1977 and was reviewed during 1983.[8] Revisions are forthcoming as of this writing. Although the general volume, ISBD (G), is the basis on which the rules in *AACR2* were constructed, ISBD (NBM) has some specific rules which differ from those in *AACR2*. It is my impression that ISBD (NBM) is not widely used in North America.

During the 18 years in which I have been involved in the cataloging of nonbook materials, the biggest problem has been terminology. Some terms were entrenched in their use by various groups; for example, librarians used *phonotape*, while audiovisual specialists preferred *audiotape*. General terms, such as *record* and *film*, were meaningless in the library context. Trade names, such as *microcard*, were to be avoided. Some words in the English language have different meanings on either side of the Atlantic; for example, *kit* in Great Britain is something one carries on one's back while camping and *pack* is a multimedia set. Fortunately, *AACR2* seems to have solved the terminology problem, although a tempest has blown up around the term *machine-readable data file*, which is the official general material designation for microcomputer software.

**Contemporary Times**

This has been a selective, and sometimes personal, brief overview of the history of nonbook cataloging. Where are we now? We have *AACR2*, which allows us to have an integrated catalog and which has been based, in part, on *Nonbook Materials: The Organization of Integrated Collections* as well as manuals emanating from the AECT and Library Association in Great Britain.[9] There are revisions to *AACR2* and numerous manuals to be used with it.

It is important to understand that a single manual cannot be all things to all libraries. Manuals are written for a particular audience and from a particular point of view. You should discover a manual's orientation before you select the one most suited to your library's catalog. As an illustration, I shall describe ours, that is, the second edition of *Nonbook Materials: The Organization of Integrated Collections.*[10]

Published in 1979, *Nonbook Materials* was written for the purpose of creating browsing collections and integrated catalogs. It was also intended to be used as a teaching tool. Since 1979 there have been many rule revisions and interpretations amending the code or its application in the field. (Author's note: I keep the book up-to-date for my students by means of an addendum sheet. If you are interested in having a copy of this addendum, please write to me.) A third edition of *Nonbook Materials* will be published when the bulk of rule revisions and interpretations affecting nonbook materials have been passed. At the moment, I anticipate publication in 1987 or 1988.

What will the future bring? Two packages of revisions to *AACR2* have been published. The third package, which will contain revisions passed at the 1983 and 1984 Joint Steering Committee for Revision of AACR (JSC—the international body responsible for the second edition of *AACR* and its continuing evolution) meetings, was published in 1986. Rule revisions and additions relating to nonbook materials in this package involve the following:

> Materials for the visually handicapped. Some librarians regard these materials as nonbook, some do not.
> Optionally, the ability to list the container and its dimensions for all materials.
> Rules for unpublished items being cataloged individually and in collections.
> The listing of one or more sound channels only if the information is readily available.

The listing of the dimensions of microfiches only if other than standard, i.e., 10.5 × 14.8 cm. JSC is moving in the direction of eliminating standard technical information from the catalog record.

Changes in the rules for uniform titles applied to popular music.

A change in the terminology used in the extent of items for stereographs, from double frames to pairs of frames.

Some changes in the rules for listing durations.

At the 1984 meeting JSC decided to recommend to *AACR2*'s publishers (i.e., the American Library Association, Canadian Library Association, and [British] Library Association) that a consolidation of the code be published in 1988. This consolidation will bring into one volume the revisions passed and the typographical errors noted to that date. It will also include revised rules for the cataloging of videodiscs, a medium which has changed technologically since 1978, and new rules for compact sound discs and microcomputer software, media which were not in library collections in 1978.

In the next decade it is probable that rules for cataloging online databases and products of electronic publishing will be developed.

Code revision from first proposal to published statement takes a minimum of two years. How does a cataloger cope with new materials in the meantime? The cataloger must understand the basic principles of *AACR2* and try to find a rule which is analagous to the problem in hand. If you do this, you should not be too far away from the final rule revision. JSC first judges all proposals as to whether they adhere to *AACR2* concepts, and secondly, seeks a comparable rule already in existence before deciding on a rule revision. It may also be wise to catalog new types of materials at the first level of bibliographic description,[11] even if the policy of the library is to do second level description, and complete the record when new rules are finally published. If you think the rules you have devised are a good idea, write to representatives of the national cataloging agency or professional association in your country.

## The Future of Nonbook Cataloging

Predictions about the more distant future are more difficult. The following quotations typify the lack of consensus among knowledgeable people. In separate essays in *Beyond "1984": The Future of Library Technical Services*, Michael Gorman, one of the editors of *AACR2*, predicts ". . . that there will never be an *AACR3*, and that the next general cataloguing code will be a manual on how to create MARC records for the national on-line network."[12] Theodore Grams expects that ". . . a new edition of the cataloguing rules, more useful and acceptable to the library community, will replace *AACR2*,"[13] and Carol Krumm and Beverly McDonald speak of ". . . the inevitability of *AACR3*."[14]

So it is with some hesitation that I add my prediction to the many already published; I shall confine it to an area with which I have had a close connection—general material designations (GMDs). The time is coming, probably very soon, when we will have to abandon GMDs. When the GMD list was first published, media fit more easily into categories, although the problem of toys was never solved satisfactorily. Now we are faced with categorizing things such as videogames. Are they videorecordings, games, or machine-readable data files? There are items which defy categorization. I have a cardboard cube which gives different metric equivalencies on each surface. It is three-dimensional, but not a model or realia, and it does not fit the definition for a chart. Future technologies will develop new, and as yet unimagined, media which may be difficult to categorize. Changing technologies will also introduce new formats into existing GMDs which may necessitate new definitions or modification of the appropriate term. This is illustrated by the advent of microcomputer software which has caused much controversy about the GMD *machine-readable data file*. As sophisticated computer programs become more common, an outdated GMD system will fall into disuse.

However, I want to inject a note of caution into this picture of the automated future. The Canadian Library Association published a study of public libraries, titled *Project Progress*, which states that 50 percent of Canadian public libraries have card catalogs.[15] It may be that the automated world will only be found in cities and large libraries. A Toronto school librarian was given funds to automate her catalog and devoted many staff hours to the project. The following year the funds were not available and so she had to return to a card catalog. Because of all the wasted effort, she says she will stick to a card catalog from now on.

There is also the problem of fads. Nonbook materials were the fad of the 1960s and 1970s; everyone was buying nonbook items whether they were useful or not. Microcomputer software may be the fad of the 1980s. I remember when electronic video recordings were introduced with such fanfare by very reputable firms. Who would have believed that they would vanish? Do you remember motion picture loop cartridges with their expensive machinery and multiple formats? An interesting article by Charles Chadwick-Healey, titled "The Future of Microforms in an Electronic Age," compares microforms favorably to videodiscs.[16] I am not suggesting that microcomputers are a passing fad or that nonbook materials were valueless. Nonbook materials have been a very important educational resource and microcomputers are playing a revolutionary role in our work and personal lives. What I am suggesting is that time and experience sorts out the ephemeral and the valuable. Careful selection now by librarians and knowledgeable use by patrons will ensure the continued significance of many nonbook materials.

### Notes

1. Charles Goodrum, *The Library of Congress* (New York: Praeger, 1974), 11.

2. Arundell Esdaile, *The British Museum Library: A Short History and Survey* (London: Allen & Unwin, 1946), 216.

3. Dorcas Fellows, *Cataloging Rules with Explanations and Illustrations,* 2nd ed. rev. and enl. (New York: H. W. Wilson, 1922), 263.

4. Library of Congress, Descriptive Cataloging Division, *Rules for Descriptive Cataloging in the Library of Congress: Phonorecords,* preliminary ed. (Washington, D. C.: LC, 1952), iii.

5. Jean Riddle, Shirley Lewis, and Janet Macdonald, *Nonbook Materials: The Organization of Integrated Collections,* preliminary ed. (Ottawa: Canadian Library Association, 1970).

6. Jean Riddle Weihs, Shirley Lewis, and Janet Macdonald, *Nonbook Materials: The Organization of Integrated Collections,* 1st ed. (Ottawa: Canadian Library Association, 1973). This endorsement was also announced in many professional journals.

7. *Anglo-American Cataloging Rules, North American Text, Chapter 12 Revised: Audiovisual Media and Special Instructional Materials* (Chicago: American Library Association, 1975); *Anglo-American Cataloging Rules, North American Text, Chapter 14 Revised: Sound Recordings* (Chicago: American Library Association, 1976).

8. International Federation of Library Associations and Institutions, Working Group on the International Standard Bibliographic Description for Non-Book Materials, *ISBD(NBM): International Standard Bibliographic Description for Non-Book Materials* (London: IFLA International Office for UBC, 1977).

9. Library Association, Media Cataloguing Rules Committee, *Non-Book Materials Cataloguing Rules: Integrated Code of Practice and Draft Revision of the Anglo-American Cataloguing Rules, British Text, Part III,* Working Paper, no. 11 (London: National Council for Educational Technology with the LA, 1973); Alma M. Tillin and William J. Quinly, *Standards for Cataloging Nonprint Materials: An Interpretation and Practical Application,* 4th ed. (Washington, D.C.: Association for Educational Communications and Technology, 1976).

10.   Jean Weihs, with Shirley Lewis and Janet Macdonald, *Nonbook Materials: The Organization of Integrated Collections*, 2nd ed. (Ottawa: Canadian Library Association, 1979).

11.   Michael Gorman and Paul W. Winkler, eds., *Anglo-American Cataloguing Rules*, 2nd ed. (Chicago: American Library Association; Ottawa: Canadian Library Association, 1978), 14–15.

12.   Michael Gorman, "Technical Services, 1984–2001 (and Before)," in *Beyond "1984": The Future of Library Technical Services*, ed. Peter Gellatly (New York: Haworth Press, 1983), 70.

13.   Theodore C. W. Grams, "Technical Services: The Decade Ahead," in *Beyond "1984*," 21.

14.   Carol R. Krumm and Beverly I. McDonald, "Libraries on the Line," in *Beyond "1984*," 118.

15.   Urban Dimensions Group, Inc., *Project Progress: A Study of Canadian Public Libraries*, prepared for the Canadian Library Association and its division The Canadian Association of Public Libraries (Ottawa: CLA, 1981), 21.

16.   Charles Chadwick-Healey, "The Future of Microforms in an Electronic Age," *Wilson Library Bulletin* 58(Dec. 1983):270–273.

# ■ Bibliographic Control Theory and Nonbook Materials

by Richard P. Smiraglia

*The foundations on which all our efforts in organizing materials are based are the principles of bibliographic control. In this chapter, Richard P. Smiraglia provides the context within which all that follows in this book may be understood.*

*For years, we have been led to believe that the unique qualities of nonbook materials made them difficult to control. With precise analyses, Smiraglia explores these unique qualities and demonstrates how the principles of bibliographic control apply to them, too. Once one has read this material and understood its explanations, nonbook formats lose their mystery. The same logical and systematic organizing principles that are applied to books fit, naturally, to information manifested in nonbook formats. The physical manifestation of a work may alter the way we perceive it, but not the way it fits into the theoretical constructs that embody all works.*

This chapter provides a brief background about bibliographic control and theory, then presents bibliographic control in general, and cataloging in particular, in terms of a theoretical construct. This construct is used to examine some of the special problems inherent in the bibliographic control of nonbook materials.

## Bibliographic Control Theory

Bibliographic control is the goal of the entire realm of activity encompassing the creation, storage, manipulation, and retrieval of bibliographic data. Bibliographic control is an integral aspect of, but is not limited to, librarianship, and is the raison d'etre of

Richard P. Smiraglia is Associate Professor of Library Administration at the University of Illinois at Urbana-Champaign, and author of *Cataloging Music: A Manual for Use with AACR2.*

documentation and information science. Bibliographic control enhances the process of communication between those who create and those who consume the creations. Without bibliographic control, there could be no free flow of information; the quality of life and indeed the development of society would suffer. Bibliographic control does not differ in substance from one type of bibliographic object to another, nor does it differ from one type of work to another. Neither the processes involved (bibliographic description, term indexing, record format, manipulation, transfer, etc.) nor the ultimate goal is material-specific. Therefore, it is not possible to separate the bibliographic control of nonbook materials—really just another class of objects—from the larger domain of "book-based" bibliographic control activity.

The term *theory* can have many definitions. At best, theory is a body of systematically organized knowledge, grounded in empirical understanding and therefore subject to refutation as a function of the shifting currents of human understanding. True theory (as distinct from the colloquial usage meaning *idea* or *principle*) enables us to analyze, predict, or otherwise explain specific phenomena. Theory is derived from the observation of phenomena. It is from theory that hypotheses can be projected, tests of which may confirm, reform, or entirely refute the original theory. The power of theory lies in our ability to use it to analyze, predict, and, therefore, find solutions to human dilemmas.

The need for fundamental or theoretical research in librarianship is much remarked upon in the literature. It is true that more theory with empirical grounding is essential to provide direction for the rapidly developing future, not only of bibliographic control, but of all library and information science. However, this is not to say that there is no theory at all. Early attempts to explain bibliographic phenomena in theoretical terms still influence the practice of bibliographic control. That these "theories" are based on common sense rather than scientific evidence may be a reflection of the current stage of development in the field of library and information science.

In libraries, bibliographic control has been referred to as "the art or skill of organizing knowledge for retrieval."[1] This is achieved through the creation, dissemination, and use of bibliographic *sources* such as enumerative bibliographies (or lists), abstracting and/or indexing services, and, of course, catalogs. Kathryn Weintraub has identified four functions that are considered appropriate for bibliographic sources. These are:

1. the finding list, or identifying function
2. the gathering function
3. the collocating function
4. the evaluative or selecting function.[2]

These functions closely resemble and can be seen to have evolved from Cutter's "Objects" for a catalog.[3] In this way, Cutter's "Objects" (i.e., principles) still underlie the development of bibliographic sources, including automated catalogs, most of which still mimic the structure of traditional card catalogs.

Patrick Wilson, in *Two Kinds of Power*,[4] sets forth a conceptual framework for bibliographic control that can be seen as the basis of a theoretical construct. He suggests the existence of two domains of bibliographic control, which he refers to as descriptive and exploitative. Descriptive control is used to organize a body of bibliographic objects. Exploitative control is the ability to make the best possible use of a body of knowledge. Wilson sees exploitative control as the superior, if unattainable, of his "two kinds of power"; descriptive control as the inferior, if more readily available.

Exploitative control is what users need. Descriptive control is what we have in our libraries to guide them. The various orderings of the objects provide pathways to understanding the relationships among the works they contain, thus offering the user some opportunities to make the best possible use of a body of knowledge. Descriptive control in this way is a precondition of exploitative control.

Wilson is not the first modern library philosopher to see bibliographic control in two domains. In 1949, Margaret Egan and Jesse Shera proposed a similar structure using different terms. They wrote of internal and external considerations. Bibliographic control can be viewed internally "as from the standpoint of the librarian and scholar who devise it and use it." It may also be viewed externally against the background of intellectual activities in general.[5]

The descriptive domain encompasses all of library cataloging, classification, and indexing; all those activities which provide an ordering of bibliographic surrogates in what we suppose to be useful ways. Refining Weintraub's observation, three functions can be defined in the descriptive domain:

1. the identifying function (enabling a user to find a particular bibliographic object)
2. the collocating function (incorporating Weintraub's "gathering and collocating" functions; collocating is defined as

"the arranging of elements in certain positions, particularly side by side"[6])
3.    the evaluative or selecting function.

This third function is the user's gateway to the exploitative domain. Without this particular element there would be little point
to bibliographic control. It is also this function which provides
the researcher with a way to evaluate the theoretical efficacy of
any given descriptive activity. To the extent that the particular
descriptive activity, such as arranging bibliographic data in a particular sequence, provides the user with evaluative information
about the object described, that activity can be seen as theoretically
grounded. To the extent that the activity is not helpful in the
evaluative function, it is therefore not efficacious in this theoretical
context.

Turning to a more direct discussion of cataloging, let us look
at some special problems that arise with nonbook materials, and
see how they fit in a general way into this theoretical context.

### Bibliographic Description

Bibliographic description is the act of transcribing and annotating
what I call the *inherent bibliographic data* about a bibliographic
object (or item) in such a way that the item itself can be identified
by reference to the description. The aim of this activity is to identify a physical object (the item) as distinct from the intellectual
entity it contains (the work). This item/work dichotomy is the
crux of many theoretical problems in bibliographic control.

The inherent bibliographic data are the statements such as title,
names, edition, publisher, etc., that can be used together to identify
an object bibliographically. To a greater or lesser extent, depending
on the type of material as well as other factors such as the economic circumstances from which it springs, these inherent bibliographic data may serve also to identify the intellectual entity
contained by the object. The description of an object, however,
may be (and often is with nonbook materials) insufficient to identify a work. Hence the philosophical separation of the acts of
bibliographic description (recording details about the object) and
providing access to the works contained by those objects.

In bibliography, this dichotomy is widely accepted. In library
cataloging, which has borrowed the tools of bibliography as a
foundation, the distinction between the object and specific intellectual entity becomes hazier. Books, and even journal articles (if

we wish to discuss abstracting and indexing services in the same context as book cataloging), tend to bear inherent bibliographic data that exactly correspond to the label that would be used to identify the specific intellectual entity. For instance, George Orwell's novel about the Spanish Civil War is titled *Homage to Catalonia*. This title identifies the intellectual entity, and whenever it appears as the title proper of a manifestation, the bibliographic description can be used to identify the work as well as the item.

Nonbook materials are another matter. Books and other printed materials (at least on the face of it) present texts. Nonbook materials, almost by definition, present more than text. A videotape or film of a novel or play is something more than the text from which it was derived. Other possibilities include a recorded performance of a musical work; an idea or a skill or technique as is the case with games, kits, etc.; a printed item, such as a map or musical score; or textual nonprinted matter, such as computer files. The point is that with nonbook materials, the inherent bibliographical data, such as those transcribed into bibliographic descriptions, are not likely to convey the notion behind the object, that is, the intellectual entity.

Nevertheless, objects are important; sometimes people want them irrespective of their content. For example, library employees may need to verify copies by matching imprints and page numbers, or scholars may need to verify publishing trends, the identification of which are dependent on precise bibliographic data. Consequently, bibliographic description remains primarily an act of transcription, intent on describing an object.

Carolyn Frost's *Cataloging Nonbook Materials* begins with a discussion of specific bibliographic concepts and their application to nonbook materials.[7] Borrowing from Frost's work, I'd like to look at the problems of choosing a chief source of information, general material designations, and the concepts of edition and publication.

Because in theory we want our catalogs to provide descriptive control of a set of bibliographical objects, we see that bibliographic descriptions should consist largely of what I have been calling the inherent bibliographic data. Where do we look for these data? If we're cataloging textual matter, we'll look on the title page. Obviously, with nonbook materials there is no equally convenient locus for the required data.

Frost discusses the concept of title page; working her way through the list of types of nonbook materials, she points out which have title-page-like data sources. Examples are motion picture title frames, music title pages, and sound recording labels. She also points to those which do not, such as kits and photographs.

Ultimately, she suggests the criteria that make title pages "attractive" (her term) as chief sources of information. These are location of the data source and fullness of the information. She states that "the title page of a book is . . . uniformly located at or near the beginning of the complete sequence of pages."[8] In sequential media, such as films, she notes a preference for information at the beginning of the sequence of images, but closest to the subject content. For example, we prefer information at the beginning of a film to information within the film, but also we prefer the frames closest to the visual content over those which may appear first, such as the brief title found on many microfilms.

The second criterion is fullness of information, "giving precedence to the source providing the most complete or comprehensive information."[9] Though an integral source is preferred, external sources, such as sound recording containers, may be preferred if they present the object as a collective entity.

There are many discussions of the general material designation (GMD) in cataloging textbooks and the journal literature because of the controversy surrounding the issue during the writing of *AACR2*. Frost characterizes the function of the medium designator as:

1. a statement of the nature of basic format of the item cataloged and thus a means of informing the user as to the type of material represented by the description
2. a description of the physical characteristic of the medium and a means of alerting the user to equipment needed to make use of the item
3. a device to distinguish different physical formats which share the same title.[10]

The common thread here is the function of informing the user sufficiently to expedite evaluation of the bibliographic data. Recalling our earlier discussion, the third function of a bibliographic source is the evaluating function—and it is the proper working of this function that most clearly allows the use of descriptive bibliographic control as a means to exploitative bibliographic control, or making the best possible use of a body of knowledge. Thus, to the extent that universal application of a medium designation enhances the performance of a descriptive source in the exploitative domain, its use would seem to be indicated in this theoretical framework.

Frost also looked for bibliographical precedence (i.e., the book title page) in her discussion of the concepts of edition and publication. I lump together edition, publication, and physical description for the purpose of this discussion because it is my opinion that, in general, all three areas suffer at present from an obscurity of purpose.

As Frost points out, the format of all three areas evolved from bibliographical precedents. There seems to be in general cataloging a trend toward using these areas to assist in the purchase of objects. Edition statements are transcribed not only when they appear on an object, but also sometimes interpolated when they do not. Occasionally, they are transcribed even when the information conveyed does not pertain to the edition. For instance, in music cataloging, statements such as "High voice," which often appear on the chief sources of songs, are transcribed as edition statements if the work has been published in versions for, say, soprano, contralto, and alto (or by analogy, tenor, baritone, and bass) voices. These are not really editions, meaning copies produced from a single set of plates (a musical term for type), as much as they are arrangements. Details of publication may be transcribed amidst extraneous information, such as the publisher's address. Physical description seems to be standardized, however, in silly ways for some materials and not particularly informative bibliographically or otherwise. We don't collate anymore, we suggest the extent of an item.

The point is that we seem to have lost any sense of bibliographic purpose in these areas. We do not provide sufficiently complete or accurate data to inform the user who is attempting to distinguish among variant manifestations of a bibliographical object. We add a lot of information that has no bibliographical purpose under the guise of "informing the user," but are the user's needs truly served?

In this theoretical context it would seem likely that the best use of these areas would be to perform the identifying and distinguishing functions within the descriptive domain. If this is so, then a better approach might be a return to transcription without interpolation in the edition and publication areas. The physical description area must be reexamined in this context to determine how best to simultaneously identify and differentiate among similar objects.

## Access to Works

Access to objects is as important as access to works. I believe that access to objects is well provided in many ways, varying from title indexes to numerical indexes such as ISBN. The focus of the remainder of this chapter is on the other half of the bibliographical dichotomy, that is, providing access to works. The problem can be divided into two segments: name and name/title access; and classification activity including subject headings.

Without a doubt, access must be provided to an authored work under headings formulated to represent both the author and the work. Further, other responsible parties must likewise be identified.[11] This satisfies the finding as well as the collocating function of the descriptive source. The growth of automated bibliographic sources, and particularly the articulation of principles of authority control, means that in the not too distant future we could begin to realize the complete separation of description and access functions. Likewise, we should be able to think of all access points as equal regardless of where they are displayed in the bibliographic record.

Authority control is viewed as another process in the descriptive domain. By providing unique identifiers (or headings), authority control enables the user to find particular works always referred to in the same way. It also allows us to gather together under a common identifier all the manifestations of a particular work. When authority work has been successful, all variant forms of a particular identifier are linked in an authority structure so that the user may be freed from the burden of knowing beforehand exactly which identifier should be used to seek a work and/or any or all of its physical manifestations.

Authority control is critical for an integrated catalog which combines differing physical manifestations of a given work in a single source. For example, the headings constructed for Margaret Mitchell's novel *Gone with the Wind* (name/title) and the film *Gone with the Wind* (uniform title) represent manifestations of the same intellectual entity. But each heading also represents a slightly different intellectual entity. Authority control, by means of links among headings (the syndetic structure), provides the user with a way to distinguish the two variants as well as to collocate (under title) the headings for each.

Similarly, subject access, where the concept of aboutness is applicable—and form access where it is not—must also be provided in sufficient detail to fulfill the gathering and evaluating functions. Subject access is particularly critical for many types of nonbook materials. Educational games, microcomputer software, realia, and some types of sound recordings exist where the creator's name or the title does not provide the most direct access to the intellectual content. These names are not likely to be well known to users who seek the information these objects contain.

Classification also fulfills the collocating function by bringing all the items with similar subject or form characteristics together on the shelf, or by bringing together under a single classification all the bibliographic records for these items. In collections that will be browsed the necessity for subject classification is assumed. As for the use of classification to organize bibliographic files, it seems to me to be much the same as the use of subject headings. Classification can be more elegant structurally and can emphasize more of the pertinent subject characteristics than current popularly used subject heading lists. But, in a structured controlled vocabulary system such as PRECIS, results similar to those obtained with classification are possible and even efficient given a sophisticated information retrieval system.

## Conclusions

Reflecting on the cataloging problems addressed in this chapter in light of the theoretical context, we've seen how in each case the purpose of a given aspect of the bibliographic record fits neatly one or more of the articulated functions of bibliographical sources. We've seen as well how these functions form the operational parameters for descriptive control and how they, in turn, enable users to approach exploitative control. I deliberately neglected to discuss the "art" of cataloging, instead emphasizing the act of transcription of inherent bibliographic data into standardized portions of the record and discussing precoordinated, strictly controlled, systematized forms of access. Nevertheless, I recognize the artistic aspect of cataloging. A bibliographic record is a surrogate for the object and its substantive content. The cataloger, before construction of the record, must decide what the object represents and how best to interpret that representation into a bibliographic record.

Nevertheless, this interpretive act must recognize the purpose inherent in the theoretical construct, which is to provide the gateway to the exploitative domain. Those responsible for the construction of the standards used to create bibliographical sources must keep this purpose always in mind. They must allow for the possibility that traditional methods do not satisfy the user's need to know and that new methods might better allow the user access to the exploitative domain. Catalogers engaged in the lonely act of interpreting one object at a time must also keep this purpose in mind so as not to obscure the intellectual entity in a maze of so-called perfect cataloging.

Frost introduces my final point, saying "standards for cataloging nonbook materials have been derived from concepts and standards developed for books. Although these concepts have had to be modified and extended, they have still served as effective models for the bibliographic description of nonbook materials."[12]

This is a natural relationship when viewed in the general theoretical context. Certainly, the data stored and manipulated in each element of the record will differ from material to material because the materials themselves differ. There is much room for improvement in the structure of the bibliographic record.

As long as future standards are influenced by an appropriate theoretical construct, the ultimate goal of control over the bibliographical universe for those who desire to exploit that universe is served. This, after all, is the essence of library and information service. And our ability to consider the bibliographic control of nonbook materials in a broader theoretical context can only expedite equivalent treatment of all materials within the bibliographic universe.

## Notes

1.   Elaine Svenonius, "Directions for Research in Indexing, Classification and Cataloging," Library Resources & Technical Services 25 (1981):88.

2.   D. Kathryn Weintraub, "The Essentials or Desiderata of the Bibliographic Record as Discovered by Research," Library Resources & Technical Services 23 (1979):392.

3.   Charles Ammi Cutter, Rules for a Dictionary Catalog, 4th ed., rewritten (Washington, D.C.: Govt. Printing Office, 1904), 12.

4.   Patrick Wilson, Two Kinds of Power: An Essay on Bibliographical Control (Berkeley: University of California Press, 1968).

5.   Jesse H. Shera and Margaret Egan, "Prolegomena to Bibliographic Control," Journal of Cataloging and Classification 5 (1949):16.

6.   Sally H. McCallum, "Some Implications of Desuperimposition," Library Quarterly 47 (1977):113.

7.   Carolyn O. Frost, Cataloging Nonbook Materials: Problems in Theory and Practice, ed. Arlene Taylor Dowell (Littleton, Colo.: Libraries Unlimited, 1983).

8.   Frost, Cataloging Nonbook Materials, 35.

9.   Frost, Cataloging Nonbook Materials, 35.

10.   Frost, Cataloging Nonbook Materials, 45.

11.   See especially Elaine Svenonius, Betty Baughman, and Mavis Molto, "Title Page Sanctity: The Distribution of Access Points in a Sample of English Language Monographs," Cataloging & Classification Quarterly 6, no. 3 (Spring 1986):3–22.

12.   Frost, Cataloging Nonbook Materials, 57.

■

## ■ Developing Nonbook
# Collections

by Sheila S. Intner

A sense of bibliocentricity among librarians should
not preclude the use of nonbook materials to meet a uniform set of
institutional objectives in any library. Sheila S. Intner believes that
nonbook materials should be collected whenever they exist in the interest areas of the public being served.

In the chapter which follows, Intner discusses collection development and acquisitions from the perspective of the nonbook materials
collector. An ardent advocate of integrated collections, Intner presents
solid evidence for the integration of collection development and acquisition activities as well. Her well-informed discussion demonstrates
ways in which administrative decisions on the organization and dissemination of materials and hardware must coincide to meet the library's service objectives. Including an explication of the particular
problems of collection development for nonbook materials, she illustrates the intimate relationship between the two processes of collection
development and acquisitions through their mutual ties into the budgeting and selector/user feedback aspects of collection management.
Like many of her colleagues in this volume, she looks forward to a
time when the role of the librarian will be to obtain needed materials,
not just to buy books.

One of the critical factors in successfully developing collections
of any kind of material involves having clear and measurable
objectives for the collection, as well as definitive knowledge of
the particular institutional environment in which it will be housed
and used. You can't develop a collection of any kind in a vacuum,
but need to relate it to the larger mission of the library and the

Sheila S. Intner is Associate Professor at the Graduate School of Library and
Information Science, Simmons College, and author of *Access to Media* and *Circulation Policy of Academic, Public, and School Libraries.*

setting in which it will exist. A collection of nonbook materials must also be related to the rest of the holdings—the entire mass of materials which library clients search, browse, and use.

This chapter is divided into two parts, the collection development part coming first and the nitty gritty acquisitions part afterward. Under the rubric of development, I want to discuss why formats should be selected, what considerations other than merely having enough budget for the purchases should be made, and how the resulting collections can be evaluated. Then, under the heading of acquisitions, I will explore the various special problems of acquiring nonbook media and some solutions that have been applied.

## Collection Development for Nonbook Materials

Many librarians are still unconvinced that the establishment of collections of materials other than books and periodicals is important or practical in their institutions. Many people have written good articles about the special attributes of nonbook media that make them worthy of our attention, including, first and foremost, Marshall McLuhan, who wrote that famous slogan, "The medium is the message."[1] In the library literature are articles by Deirdre Boyle, Wesley Doak, Ron Hagler, Kandy Brandt, Angie LeClerq, and others. They mention attributes such as the immediacy of nonbook media presentations, the subtleties that visual media provide for viewers, the appeal of nontextual formats for nonreaders who may be visually handicapped or dyslexic or just unable to read easily and well, and the ability of an audiovisual presentation to illustrate complex processes or procedures in a way that words cannot imitate.

The fact is that you have to go all the way back to an examination of the mission of your library to decide whether there is a need for it to establish and develop any particular collection. Wesley Doak said some years ago in an article in *Library Quarterly* that there shouldn't be any such thing as a nonbook material collection or a nonbook material librarian, but that all members of the library staff should be equally knowledgeable about the materials and adept at their use, while the materials themselves should be dispersed to the shelves wherever their content was appropriate.[2] However, thanks to our habit of adhering to traditional administrative divisions, Doak's ideal is unlikely to become a widespread phenomenon, and separate nonbook collections are here to stay.

Once upon a time libraries would decide to have nonbook media, as if you could go out and order, "One hundred nonbook medias, please." They might have based the decision on a desire to be progressive or innovative, or to follow the advice being given in the library literature by media proponents throughout the 1960s (when there were federal dollars available). They might actually have had a demand from their clients, though this might not have received the greatest attention despite our claims to be sensitive to the needs of the public. They might have had a staff member with a great interest in one of the nonbook media formats. They might have used a proposal as a means of obtaining additional funds for new programs. (One of the saddest things about library funding is the relative ease with which new programs may receive approval, while the continuing support and strengthening of existing programs will often go begging, regardless of their value or significance to the public.)

Elementary and secondary school libraries were in the forefront of nonbook materials collection development—using federal funds for materials—though they rarely included provision for processing the materials properly for use. Public libraries followed along behind schools, and academic and research libraries lagged far behind both, not having the benefits of federal funding until much later as well as lacking the push from either their clients or colleagues to collect nonbook materials. If you examine articles from the late 1930s and 1940s, the typical academic library discussion of nonbook materials was in the context of a teachers' college or school of education within a university. The disciplines of art, music, and medicine also were early consumers of nonbook materials in the academic world, though only of their related individual forms, that is, slides, pictures, and photographs; scores and sound recordings; and laboratory slides, etc., respectively.

Most of the early articles about nonbook materials are set in school libraries, with a sprinkling of public library accounts. The significance of this fact is that as large academic and research libraries emerged in the late 1950s as the leaders of the profession and as they began to exert their influence, the question of the place of nonbook materials in librarianship slowly began to recede.

By 1970, less and less notice was being taken of nonbook materials' issues, especially compared to the 1960s when attention was at its zenith. Since 1980, mention of nonbook materials' problems has been sparse, and usually directed only at the newest formats, that is, video and computer software. We are now concerned with other, and more pressing, problems, such as how to deal with budget cuts and fiscal retrenchment, and how to auto-mate our libraries. "To media or not to media" is no longer the question. The fact that surveys throughout the 1970s demonstrated that no sector of the library world (public, school, academic, and research) met even minimum standards set by professional orga-nizations for nonbook collections and services was shoved aside by more urgent matters. Boyd Ladd reported on a national study sponsored jointly by the Association for Educational Communi-cations and Technology and the National Commission on Libraries and Information Science conducted in 1975.[3] It showed that even the public schools, which had amassed some one million nonbook items at that time and were the most avid collectors for the longest period of time, had a long way to go to meet the standards (cal-culated by Ladd and his colleagues at one *billion* nonbook items). Furthermore, Ladd's study demonstrated the imbalance in the distribution of these materials, with more affluent urban areas owning far more materials proportionally than the less affluent rural areas of the nation.

Since every library collection should be based on the needs of the institution's clientele, materials of all sorts should be consid-ered in light of these needs. How can any librarian worth the title consider a music, art, or popular culture collection complete with-out appropriate nonbook materials? How can a library in a medical school teaching surgery be considered fully stocked without videotapes of surgical procedures? How can a modern journalism program exist without collections in their library of documentary films, video news, and so forth? And, if a public library serves children, can they afford to be without games—especially video games—and toys? Do adults want dress patterns, microcomputer software, films and videorecordings, exercise records, language tapes, framed prints of paintings, and tools, as well as a good read?

The issue is not whether nonbook materials should be included in a library's holdings, but what works in which formats offer the best collection for the needs of the users, not just what books are available in a subject or interest area. To succeed in establishing a special emphasis collection on Shakespearean drama, is it enough to buy the books about Shakespeare's plays and editions of the works themselves without also offering sound recordings, videorecordings, and/or films of staged productions? If public li-braries want to serve their communities as repositories of local history materials, should they include photographs, drawings, and oral history recordings as well as printed and manuscript materials of historical importance? Is it more effective service to buy me-diocre novels instead of good videoplays? Today, some of our best dramatists write plays first for television and only later are their works published in print. How many *Star Trek* storybooks are purchased by libraries and circulated widely until they fall apart, while the librarians don't even think of buying the same stories in their original video formats?

The mix of books and nonbooks in a collection or subject area ought to be dictated by the likelihood people will use one or another format and the relative availability of quality items in all media. If there are goals of format balance, they ought to be made on the basis of something other than tradition, and I suggest that it be use and demand that govern the allocation.

## Factors Affecting Collection Development Policies

Formats should be selected because they are used. Many libraries report that they can't satisfy the demand for videorecordings, yet they don't consider switching book allocations to video despite the knowledge that many of the books purchased will not circulate more than once or twice. They just limit the use of video to an absurd degree. Items within a format should be selected because they are appropriate to the subject or interest areas of users and they are consistent with the criteria for selection of the library. Even when a library's budget will not cover the purchase of all the good books in a subject area, other formats should be included if they furnish a high-quality and diverse kind of material for the public. Nonbook materials should not be purchased from leftover funds, but should be selected on the basis of their potential contribution to the overall collection. Unfortunately, the typical administrative pattern of separating the nonbook material from other subject or discipline-oriented departments, and tying selection to each department, negates the possibility that this can occur naturally. Of course, a library may exist in an area where no one listens to the radio or television, goes to the movies, plays a stereo, or owns a tape recorder, but I'm not sure where that would be.

Several considerations should accompany a decision to develop collections of nonbook materials. Administrative decisions must be made about the policies that will govern the materials, such as how they are processed, cataloged, and classified (e.g., will they circulate or be reference only? will they be shelved on open or closed stacks? and so on). Another decision involves hardware. Librarians must decide whether to obtain the necessary hardware to use the materials in-house, to circulate along with the software, or only to deal with the software.

A third decision is both administrative and hardware-related:

what, if any, charges will accompany the establishment and operation of these materials and equipment? When it comes to microcomputer software, libraries are finding they can charge the public for using the computers on which the software runs and people are literally standing in line to pay. Even such minimal charges as fifty cents an hour add up when multiplied by the sixty or more hours a week that a public library stays open. When that figure is multiplied by three or four machines, it adds up to $90 a week for an institution with three computers operating sixty hours a week. Over a year's time that will total $4,500, enough to pay for a pretty fancy microcomputer system. After a year, any further use the library gets from the system is gravy. In the case of tape recorders, film and slide projectors, microscopes, phonographs, video players, etc., the charges might cover the cost of maintenance, or in all cases, the library could decide to absorb the costs involved, charging only for repairs or damages incurred outside the library.

This may all seem simplistic, but these decisions were once made for the book collections—what will circulate and what won't; how should books be processed; will the library charge for some books, for example, rental collections; will the stacks be open or closed; and so on. In my opinion, the same rules should apply to nonbook materials as to the books in a particular interest area. By that I mean if music books and scores circulate and are on open stacks, then recorded music (and today, this involves video as well as traditional sound-only discs, cassettes, cartridges, etc.) probably should be handled in the same way. If printed music materials are limited in some way, then recordings should be limited accordingly. Decision makers must weigh the relative advantages of open or closed access, circulation or reference status, and so on, for all materials in a collection, not merely the books or the films.

The last issue to be covered here in connection with collection development of nonbook media is about evaluation of the collections and subsequent decisions to weed or purchase materials. You are undoubtedly familiar with the ways librarians evaluate their book collections. They may compare their holdings with a respected bibliography or book of recommended titles. They may measure the number of volumes and divide by the population served. They may examine circulation statistics and relate these to population served. They may compare the titles held in a subject area with those of similar institutions known to be strong in this particular area. All of these are accepted methodologies for evaluating book collections.

But how do we normally evaluate collections of nonbook materials? Do we compare against "mediagraphies?" Do we compare against other institutions' strong collections? Do we divide circulation by population? Or do we divide total holdings by population according to a preset formula as our criterion of sufficiency? Do we weed nonbook collections using the same criteria as for book collections? If we are in school or academic libraries, do we immediately buy new nonbook materials when courses are added to the curriculum or are we satisfied with checking off desired titles in *Books for College Libraries* or *Choice* or *Library Journal*? Do we evaluate the nonbook materials in our collections against other collections with similar curricula or reputations for strength in this subject? Do we discard items that supported subjects no longer taught or taught differently? How much thought is involved before you actually throw out a film, a video, or a sound recording?

I submit that, in public libraries at least and perhaps in others as well, there are few media collections that are regularly evaluated either quantitatively (i.e., do we have enough titles/copies?) or qualitatively (i.e., do we have the best/right titles for our needs?). Furthermore, no one owns enough material to throw out large quantities of truly marginal items because the collections would appear depleted. Thus, in the public library where I worked as music librarian, many scratched and unused titles moldered on the shelves because it sounded so nice to say we had 20,000 discs in our collection of recorded sound. If I had weeded out all the items that had not circulated for, say, two years or had visible scratches, I believe we would have removed between 2,000 and 3,000 items. While this would not have been reckless endangerment of the collection, it would not have looked very good on the annual statistics to which this library's board was devoted in its appraisal of services rendered. I suspect the same is true of libraries in schools, colleges, and universities. Only in research libraries and archives can one make a case for keeping unused materials indefinitely, but even in these special types of repositories, there is no excuse for not evaluating collections.

To sum up the discussion of collection development, there are five main points:

1.  The same institutional objectives should be served by all materials. Book and nonbook collections in a subject area, interest area, or discipline should be coordinated.
2.  Nonbook materials should be purchased if they exist in the interest areas of the public being served. They should

not be purchased so the library can have "media" to prove how "progressive" it is, though if selected properly even this misplaced motivation might prove a boon to the public.

3. The same selectors should order a variety of quality items in all formats to satisfy a diversity of users with, literally, infinite needs. A nonbook librarian cannot possibly have the expertise to choose materials equally well in all the disciplines. Subject bibliographers are supposed to have expertise in their subject areas—not only for choosing books—and it is they who should do the selection for nonbook materials, too. (A spinoff benefit of having these librarians do the selection may be that they will be aware of the existence of nonbook titles in their areas of specialization and will utilize them more often and more effectively.)

4. Administrative decisions regarding the organization and dissemination of the materials as well as hardware associated with their use must be made to coincide with the library's overall service objectives.

5. Nonbook collections should be regularly evaluated and weeded according to the same criteria applied to books. The excellence or weakness of the collections should be determined and addressed in a manner consistent with the library's goals and objectives.

## The Acquisition of Nonbook Materials

The first of many problems with which the nonbook acquisitions librarian has to deal is the very likely case that this operation is separated from the rest of the library's acquisitions operations. When we consider shifting from printed books to a nonbook format for the same item, for example, microform backfiles of serials or sets of literature in microform, what problems will it create for the neat divisions we have come to expect, including serials, monographs, microforms, audiovisuals, etc.? The processes of acquisitions are the same for all media. The nonbook librarian has to verify the existence of materials for purchase, just as books must be verified. Catalog(s) must be checked to see if the item is already owned. Funds must be made available for payment when the material arrives. A dealer must be selected unless the item is purchased directly from its producer. All the other acquisitions tasks are performed for nonbook as well as book materials. Separation of the nonbook acquisitions from the department specifically organized to operate most efficiently, with personnel trained to do the work most skillfully, means that other staff—probably just one or two overworked nonbook librarians—will have to do the work of a whole department for the materials presenting the largest number of exceptions to the rules.

The second problem that must be confronted, no matter who is responsible for nonbook acquisitions or in which department it is done, is the enormous variety of format types subsumed under the umbrella heading *nonbook*, each with a set of producers, distributors, hardware needs, and subformats. There is no nonbook industry; there are many industries producing totally different kinds of things. The kind of product uniformity that all librarians expect from books does not exist among the media or even among items coming from competing producers within a particular medium.

Although this lack of interchangeability seems to be particularly bad in the newer formats, such as computer software and videorecordings, it exists in older and more stable industries, too. Take, for example, the sound recording industry, where there are four relatively popular storage forms—disc, cassette tape, cartridge tape, and reel-to-reel tape—as well as additional types found with less frequency in ordinary libraries, such as sound pages, cylinders, rolls, and wires. Each storage medium within the group is divided by other distinctions, such as the size of the disc or tape and the speed with which it is played back, multiplying the number of forms even further. Now there are also analog and digital recordings and compact discs read by lasers. No one knows what new subformats will emerge in the future.

Sound recordings represent only one group. If you add to it all the other nonbook forms collected by libraries and included in the cataloging rules—cartographics, music, motion pictures, video, graphics, three-dimensional materials, computer-readable materials, and microforms—a formidable number of different kinds of materials have to be considered and understood by the librarian trying to buy them. And we can multiply all of this by two if we count the division between monographs and serials.

Although the process of purchasing materials in any of these groups is basically the same, the purchasers and, certainly, the collection developers, too, must do four things:

1. They need to learn about the differing physical attributes, capabilities, and requirements of the various formats.

2.  They must be able to identify the producers, manufacturers, and distributors in each industry.
3.  They have to gather the necessary bibliographic data as well as subject and evaluative information needed for selection, verification, and ordering of individual items.
4.  They must manage the budgeting for purchase, processing, and maintenance.

(During the 1970s, several seminars were held to discuss the management and use of nonbook materials; the conclusions reached unanimously recommended that reviews of nonbook material titles be made available more readily, preferably online. Although everyone agreed it was important, there is no evidence that the recommendation had any impact.[4])

No one doubts this is a formidable task for an acquisitions librarian, but there are several reasons why it bears consideration. First, the acquisitions department should have the most efficient systems and concentration of skilled workers for the task. Second, the acquisitions officer also monitors the ongoing expenditures of various funds, notifying the appropriate department when materials are held up, go out of print, or are otherwise unavailable as expected. If nonbook materials are separate from books, there is no easy way to rearrange purchases and move the dollars from books to films or vice versa to reflect the availability of different formats at different times. Surely, there is value for a music department to know that a shipment of sound recordings is not going to arrive in time for a particular budget year so that the money may be used to obtain scores, videorecordings of the same works, or books that might otherwise not have been purchased. Third, many vendors supply a variety of materials, especially those who cater to lower-level schools, and more might be persuaded to do so if their customers would buy them. This could certainly ease the burden for everyone, and spread the vendors' profits over a larger volume of more diverse materials. (Just as an aside, consider this conundrum: In hard times, businesses either specialize or diversify to improve their positions. There are good arguments for both alternatives. Since library vendors seem to be facing hard times, perhaps they should consider either specializing in particular interest areas, carrying all formats in the ones selected, or diversifying and carrying all materials in all interest areas.)

Some librarians do develop all collections, purchase everything, and appreciate the problems and virtues of all materials. But most budgets are divided into funds for books, funds for serials, and funds for nonbook materials, occasionally divided by each format or subformat. So it seems quite natural to divide the acquisitions responsibilities the same way. The problem is that it fragments a set of duties and tasks that should interact closely to produce the best overall collections. Even when one person does all the acquisitions work, that person often cannot move funds earmarked for books or films or posters or games to another format, say, microcomputer software. Budgets are normally set up to allocate $x$ dollars to books, $y$ dollars to scores, $z$ dollars to software, etc. The acquisitions librarian will know, before anyone else, which materials are not going to arrive, but though the same title/work, intellectually speaking, might be available in another medium, it cannot be purchased to replace the original order without moving to another allocation.

Perhaps if acquisitions librarians accustomed to working with books and using such tools as *Books in Print* were to work with other formats, they would revolt, demonstrating against producers of nonbook materials until such producers quite literally got their act together into a similar *Media in Print*. Very few of the formats have such comprehensive acquisitions tools as do books. There are some filmographies, discographies, and other medium-specific tools as well as a few cross-media works with varying degrees of coverage. But most nonbook librarians collect vast numbers of producers' catalogs, distributors' lists, and advertised offerings from all sorts of sources (even retail stores which give no discounts, but carry hard-to-find materials wanted by libraries).

Verifying the existence of a nonbook title may be an exercise in futility because there is no citation uniformity in the listings of different sources (or the same sources at different times). Titles may vary, translations may differ. Some filmographies give directors main entry while others list by title, and still others have subject or some other element as their primary entry point, just as some discographies list by performer, some by label, and others by composers or titles. Pinning down the actual date of issue of a kit or filmstrip is not always easy when producers or distributors repackage it to make it resalable after the initial demand is over. The acquisitions librarian or selector may not realize until an item arrives with a lovely new box, new title, and new blurb that it is the same filmstrip or kit purchased years before in another form.

Wouldn't it be nice to be able to order all nonbook material with ISBNs? True, some kinds are assigned unique identifiers which may or may not mimic ISBNs, and, after all, some book publishers do not participate in the ISBN program, but wouldn't it be wonderful if most of the things we buy for libraries had them? Your lobbying is definitely in order. As more and more institutions automate their acquisitions, it will become apparent that the purchase of nonbook materials is seriously hampered by being outside the control of a well-organized, closely knit distribution system. Furthermore, we suffer from a lack of direction on the part of such comprehensive collectors of books as the Library of Congress and our greatest academic research libraries. If these institutions were comprehensive collectors of nonbook materials, they might clamor for more efficient methods of identifying individual items, which could then be used by all librarians to locate, verify, and purchase them.

To recapitulate, I see five main problems plaguing the acquisition of nonbook materials. First, it is often separated from the acquisition process for books and thus from the accompanying benefits resulting from integrating all purchasing into one efficient department. Second, there is a multiplicity of formats subsumed under the umbrella heading *nonbook*, with its implication of uniformity. Third, special dealers are needed for various formats instead of being able to use the same ones from which books are purchased. Fourth, there is a lack of comprehensive, uniform, standardized multimedia tools modeled after *Books in Print*, as well as the problems of identifying a particular item from the jumble of producers' and distributors' catalogs, mediagraphies, and promotional literature. And fifth, there is a lack of such aids to identification and purchase as ISBNs.

## Conclusion

There is little doubt that the general bibliocentricity of libraries makes the task of acquiring nonbook materials more difficult than it has to be. This bibliocentricity translates into low budgets, less efficient procedures, and an absence of uniform standards, tools, and technical assistance from producers and distributors. An effective nonbook materials acquisitions librarian is as scarce as hen's teeth and a hundred times more valuable. The two processes of collection development and acquisitions are intimately related through their mutual ties into library budgets and feedback mechanisms to selectors and users. Much can be gained by examining the library's own goals and objectives, and then determining how best to fulfill them without relegating any valid information medium to last place. The job of acquisitions librarian, then, will be to obtain needed materials, not just to buy books.

## Notes

1.  Marshall McLuhan, *Understanding Media, the Extensions of Man* (New York: McGraw-Hill, 1964), 126.

2.  Wesley Doak, "Administrative Problems and Their Solutions," *Library Quarterly* 45 (Jan. 1975):60.

3.  Boyd Ladd, *National Inventory of Library Needs, 1975: Resources Needed for Public and Academic Libraries and Public School Library/Media Centers* (Washington, D.C.: National Council on Library and Information Science, 1977).

4.  See James W. Brown, *Nonprint Media Information Networking: Status and Potentials* (Stanford, Calif.: ERIC Clearinghouse on Information Resources, 1976), 60.

■

# ■ Using Policy Statements to Define and Manage the Nonbook Collection

by Hugh A. Durbin

*In this short chapter, Hugh A. Durbin, a noted school librarian, challenges us to integrate not only our book and nonbook materials but also our administrative skills. Good management for book and nonbook collections begins with the adoption of good planning and policy statements. Policies must be formed with knowledge of user needs and the purposes and resources of each individual library. They should be flexible, up-to-date, and innovative.*

Policy statements serve as the basis for planning, budgeting, and providing staff with a guide for day-to-day activities. They inform the public, define expectations, and should enlist support. Policy safeguards against falling prey to fads, but allows for some experimentation. Policy may not exist in a single document, but rather may be scattered throughout various pronouncements, memos, and manuals of the library. Policy must be flexible, adaptable when necessary, and must recognize the multimedia nature of the library.

In Columbus we have policy statements on library learning centers. After adoption by the board, they became the chief instruments in developing the library learning center and have been useful as we added new technologies, such as microcomputers, in our schools.

Policy is never absolute, but dynamic—an ongoing process, like living with another person. Its basic premise rests on the idea that information is stored in many forms, each of which has merit for some user segment or for meeting specific objectives.

We must start with a theory of what our library is and let it

Hugh Durbin is Director of Media Services for the Columbus, Ohio, public school system. He is a school library representative to the OCLC User Council.

determine practice. Theory will always be the foundation on which practice is built. Practice may be static; it may do well with what it knows. It has, however, no principles for dealing with what it doesn't know. Practice cannot adapt readily in a changing environment and may get sidetracked in efforts to cope with constantly changing demands.

Policy statements should lead to greater equity between book and nonbook resources. It can be difficult to determine equity since it is usually viewed from one's own perspective. Statements should address the functions of selection, acquisitions, cataloging, processing, circulation, and the care and handling of materials. Nonbook materials should receive equal treatment in all these areas. From my perspective, management of nonbook materials is not a single or separate aspect of library administration, organization, and management. It is part of every area and relates to all other aspects of library administration and nearly every component of the library operation. These components are:

1. goal or mission
2. objectives
3. budget
4. acquistion, cataloging, processing
5. circulation
6. reference
7. facilities
8. staffing or personnel.

At times an administrator may focus on one or several issues that relate to nonbook materials, but it should be done only with an awareness of all the other materials in the library and with the single purpose of solving a specific issue related to that medium or those media.

Information is packaged in many formats. Each has a particular value or worth in conveying information and contributes uniquely to the total program. Each medium tends to impose its own requirements on management. Though we must generalize whenever we can, we should not neglect what must be special.

No matter what type of library, key questions are:

1. Management for whom?
   Define our users, their needs, their expectations; answers will differ, depending on the library, the institution, or the community.

2.  Management with what resources?
    Define our collections and services.
3.  Management for what purposes?
    Are collections intended for use? Is accessibility to be max-
    imized? Is preservation an issue? Often these issues con-
    flict.

## Selection Policy

Many policies have been written with the idea that one need only
insert the word *nonbook* in order to give equal status to these
materials; but each format has individual characteristics and demands different criteria or basis of selection than the others. Each
medium makes its own contribution as a carrier of information,
and should be judged accordingly. There are special considerations as well, such as protection of copyright in the use of microcomputer software. One must learn whether it differs from the
copyright protections accorded to authors of books. (In Columbus,
we are circulating software and require that borrowers sign a
pledge that they will not make illegal copies. The school will
confiscate any such copies if they are found.)

Producers' catalogs do not always give us what we expect.
However, we get back what we invest in the time and effort spent
reading them. Whoever does the selection must be knowledgeable.
This is one area in which staff capabilities are critical.

## Staffing Policy

Staffing varies greatly and no one particular pattern exists. Small
libraries have one or two persons who serve as handlers of all
materials and are expected to know each kind. Large institutions
tend to have specialists or experts for nonbook materials. Although
providing high-quality service, this pattern unfortunately leads to
the isolation of nonbook services and a lack of communication
with other departments as well as struggles to build one's own
turf.

The skills of handling nonbook materials, retrieving information about them, and operating any necessary equipment are for-
eign to many librarians. This has a detrimental effect on the quality
of library service to patrons. Effective, ongoing in-service programs are needed to educate the staff. One suggestion is to devise
ways to involve staff with nonbook materials.

**Shelving and Housing Policy**

Shelving and housing should be determined with regard to the materials, their use, and users. The question is not whether to physically integrate the materials, but which to integrate and why—or for what purposes—and then how and when. An all-encompassing "yes" or "no" would constitute an abrogation of our professional responsibilities.

The primary reason for integrating shelving has been to promote the use of materials and provide greater accessibility. Research supports such conclusions, but practice also focuses on its cost. If extra funds are not available for repackaging items to fit on the shelves or for redesigning storage space, we must look for other ways to promote accessibility. One way is to include all materials in the catalog, whether a card catalog, a computerized one, or a book catalog. There may be a need for special catalogs in addition.

There are other ways to promote awareness. Some of these include the use of bulletin boards and signs placed in strategic places. Another retrieval aid is using the same classification scheme for all materials, both book and nonbook. These decisions must be made locally, but the priority should be to make it as easy as possible for the user to get the nonbook item.

All library materials must be stored in ways that will maximize their acceptability and enhance their usability as well as prevent unnecessary deterioration from dust, heat, light, and other deleterious elements. Accountability must be established and steps taken to prevent theft. Shelvers need to be accurate in maintaining order on the shelves. After all, a misshelved item might just as well not be in the collection. If necessary, special storage containers should be used for delicate formats, such as motion pictures and microcomputer software.

There are difficulties in attempting to store various formats on uniform bookshelves. In some formats, each item is of a different size, for example, art prints. In others, the shapes are irregular, very small or very large, etc.

Nonbook materials probably should be distributed, to some extent, throughout the library. In one alternative school program in Oak Park (Illinois), "pods" containing nonbook materials are located in prominent places near related book materials, for example, oral history tapes in the history section. The incorporation of nonbook materials where they enhance book collections would probably go far to improve the attitudes of some of our colleagues.

A basic problem is determining a fair amount of space for nonbook collections and services. Merely dividing available space into equally sized portions does not necessarily accord each format its proper share. In addition, deployment of equipment should optimize use of the materials, especially if they are distributed through the library.

Nonbook resources usually require equipment for use and often there are special environmental considerations. This adds another dimension to the operation.

Good management requires:

1. an up-to-date inventory which includes records on each machine, brand, and location
2. a supply of parts that wear out frequently, such as projector light bulbs
3. maintenance and repair
4. budgeting for initial purchase and replacement
5. staff training for utilization or operation
6. storage space as well as space for the use of the equipment.

Flexibility in the use of space must be considered. The same space can be used for many activities.

# ■ Cooperation and Networking: Are There Differences for Nonbook Materials?

by Lizbeth Bishoff

*Librarians have accepted the fact that no one institution can collect every item its clients might need. The gap between what a library can acquire and what the people it serves wish to obtain has been widening for some years under the twin pressures of increasing financial constraint and burgeoning information production. For printed monographs and serials, cooperation and networking—particularly computer-based networking—are providing a solution to the dilemma. Lizbeth Bishoff encourages us to apply the same solution to the rest of our collections.*

*In this chapter, Bishoff incisively examines attitudes of library staff members toward networking for their nonbook materials and the basic requirements for drawing these materials into the mainstream of effective networking. She asks us to evaluate how our own perceptions affect our responses to networking for nonbook material. It is something like evaluating our first reaction to a glass half full of water. Do we see it as half full or half empty? For the benefit of library clients everywhere, she asks us to be positivists and shows us how to accomplish it.*

Investigating the role of nonbook materials in the total networking picture, I discovered that sharing was so limited that I questioned how I could write on the subject. On closer inspection, however, it appears there is great potential for sharing of nonbook materials, but a number of barriers must be eliminated before that potential can be realized. We need to change people's attitudes regarding the sharing of nonbook materials. We need to treat nonbook materials equally in terms of bibliographic description, entry into automated databases, and delivery. Where necessary, we need to

Lizbeth Bishoff is Principal Librarian at Pasadena (Calif.) Public Library, with responsibility for support services, including automated systems and technical services. She is a winner of the Esther J. Piercy award for excellence.

43

adjust local practices to accommodate the lending and borrowing of these materials. On a state and national level, we, as the information purveyors, need to stop treating nonbook materials differently. Only then will library users come to accept nonbook materials as vehicles carrying information, but in a different format.

Before I can discuss improving resource sharing of nonbook materials, the concept of resource sharing should be defined and past efforts at sharing nonbook resources reviewed.

## Concepts of Resource Sharing

In an article on resource sharing in the *Encyclopedia of Library and Information Science*, Allen Kent quotes Douglas Bryant, past director of the Harvard University Library, on the role of collection development in libraries:

> Through all the centuries since the Alexandrian Library, the aim of librarians and the hope of scholars has been to amass in a single library all the resources for research in any branch of knowledge. . . . This doctrine of self-sufficiency is finally coming to be realized for what it is—a will-o-the-wisp. We are seeing at last the gradual abandonment of this creed . . . sharing of holdings among libraries is increasingly accepted as an ineluctable necessity and the only realistic means of providing the full range of resources. . . . To be effective, it goes without saying that access to materials not available in one's own library must be reasonably quick and altogether reliable.[1]

We recognize that Bryant was referring to what we currently call resource sharing. From this definition, we derive the following goals:

1.  to provide the library user with access to more materials and services
2.  to provide the same service at lower cost, or, greater service at the same or lower cost than if furnished by an individual library acting alone.

In reality, inflation and budget reductions are the primary forces motivating resource sharing; however, cutbacks alone don't make sharing work. Kent notes that to make sharing work libraries must have resources to share, librarians must have a willingness to share them, and a plan must be devised to accomplish the task.[2] Resource sharing of print materials is commonplace in today's libraries. We need to implement programs to permit similar sharing of nonbook materials.

The Association of Research Libraries' survey, *A Study of the Characteristics, Costs, and Magnitude of Interlibrary Loans in Academic Libraries*,[3] studied the sharing of a variety of materials: periodicals; monographs; theses and dissertations; and nonbook materials, including films, sound recordings, maps, pictures, and microforms. The survey indicated that 91.7 percent of the libraries surveyed borrowed theses, 38 percent borrowed sound recordings, and 45 percent borrowed maps. In contrast, 75 percent were willing to lend theses (either the original or a copy); however, only 17.4 percent would lend sound recordings and 32 percent would lend maps. Interestingly, the survey doesn't address the significant discrepancy between the concomitant willingness to borrow and reluctance to lend. One might point out that the findings of ARL surveys have limited application to other types of libraries; ARL libraries do not place the same emphasis on nonbook collections as do other academic institutions. However, the issue is moot when one notes that even these libraries were willing to lend and borrow nonbook items that they had, however small the collections.

Catherine Pinion's 1980 survey, titled *The Interlending and Availability of Audiovisual Materials in the UK*, reported that 91 percent of the respondents anticipated that interlibrary loan demand for nonbook materials would be low or nonexistent.[4] Further, only 21 percent indicated willingness to request nonbook materials on loan.

Although they take different approaches, both surveys illustrate a reluctance on the part of librarians to consider nonbook materials in the realm of resource sharing, either for borrowing or lending. How, then, do we attempt to achieve the National Commission on Library and Information Science's (NCLIS) goal of access to all needed resources to satisfy individuals' educational, working, cultural, and leisure time needs and interests regardless of their location, social or physical condition, or level of intellectual achievement?[5] We cannot believe that we have met the needs of information consumers if, as information providers, we eliminate a vast portion of the universe of resources from the consumers' reach.

The question facing us seems to be: Why aren't nonbook materials taking their proper place in the world of resource sharing?

## Problems of Identifying Nonbook Materials

The first, and probably the most important, reason nonbook materials are not shared centers around the difficulty of identifying what exists and who owns it. Most libraries currently have a two-step approach to this problem. The first step involves identifying the materials that would best meet the users' needs and/or verifying the existence of a specific item. The second step involves determining who owns it. Automation, however, is changing this into a one-step process. Entry of book and nonbook materials into online union catalogs (or a COM byproduct) furnishes immediately available information on a variety of materials held in many different libraries. Databases such as OCLC, RLIN, and WLN are perceived as national-level union catalogs containing information on resources in all formats. Locally, many databases supporting circulation systems are becoming online union catalogs providing bibliographic information as well as information on the availability of the item. The role in resource sharing played by these systems will be explored later in greater detail.

Identifying those nonbook materials that are available is difficult at best. The lack of a *Media in Print* that provides a comprehensive list of all nonbook materials currently available contributes to the problem. Nonbook librarians frequently must consult a variety of tools with varying coverage to gather the necessary data to acquire materials. Online union catalogs have the potential for integrating data for all formats, as well as materials that are in and out of print. Major problems in identifying these materials begin with bibliographic description. These difficulties are cited in all articles dealing with access to nonbook materials. *Problems in Bibliographic Access to Nonprint Materials*, the report of Project Media Base, describes a survey distributed to 200 American libraries.[6] Of 43 responding libraries, most (i.e., 24) held fewer than 5,000 nonbook titles; however, three libraries held 200,000 titles or more, and the two largest collections had half a million nonbook titles each. For cataloging, 38 percent used the *Anglo-American Cataloging Rules (AACR)* and 18 percent used the Association for Educational Communication and Technology's (AECT) *Standards.*[7] For subject headings, 32 percent used *Library of Congress Subject Headings* and 15 percent used *Sears List of Subject Headings.* Regarding their systems of encoding the data, 30 percent reported compatibility with the MARC format, but only 5 (11.6 percent) used the MARC format itself.

The Project Media Base report explains the lack of standardization. Nearly half of the libraries in the survey did not use a nationally recognized standard for bibliographic description of their nonbook materials. Seventy percent of the nonlibrary, nonbook databases did not employ MARC. This lack of standardization was attributed to the absence of coordinated methods for developing rules for the description of nonbook materials. Sheila Intner's *Access to Media* traces the history of bibliographic standards, showing an increasing awareness of the need for standardization of the description of nonbook materials, moving from *AACR* and the various editions of AECT's *Standards* through the development of International Standard Bibliographic Descriptions (ISBDs) and MARC formats for all materials, culminating in the second edition of *AACR—AACR2*, an integrated code. Application of the ISBD structure to nonbook and cartographic materials and its incorporation into *AACR2* "resolved some of the problems of media cataloging. . . ."[8]

Ongoing development of the MARC format has also contributed to the process. Originally developed for books, MARC formats were developed for serials, films, manuscripts, maps, music (including sound recordings and musical scores), and, most recently, machine-readable data files. (There is also a MARC format for authority records.) MARC II was intended to provide a single format capable of containing bibliographic information for all forms of materials.[9] Ideally, development of these formats should have been coordinated. In response to critical needs, one specialized format at a time was developed. As the formats grew in complexity and increased in number, attempts to maintain consistency became more difficult. A similar pattern occurred during creation of the ISBDs resulting, eventually, in the writing of an ISBD-General with which all other ISBDs are slowly being brought into compliance. The lack of consistency in the various MARC formats resulted from their development by material specialists. John Attig wrote: "In recent years, however, the trend has been toward large integrated databases, toward multimedia collections and catalogs, and toward consistency in bibliographic description. The ISBDs and *AACR2* are monuments to this trend toward integration."[10]

Attig goes on to say: "Different types of records should not be treated differently in the MARC format if they do not need to be treated differently by their users. . . ."[11] The advent of multi-formatted systems makes consistency of content of records across formats a definite advantage. Attig proposes further work on the *MARC Formats for Bibliographic Data*. While this document contains many consistently defined content designators for all formats, "MFBD does not yet constitute a single format . . . but rather one to be used in any bibliographic record where it is appropriate."[12] Inconsistencies remain in format terminology, usage, and definitions, but with appropriate changes a single format could be realized. Artificial barriers within the format, not those imposed by the medium, would largely disappear.

Clearly, the availability and use of a single MARC format would result in greater consistency in bibliographic description of all materials, easing efforts to identify and share nonbook materials. The MARC format is still book-oriented; however, progress is being made and were Attig's suggestions to be implemented, the remaining bias would be significantly reduced.

Earlier, I made reference to *AACR2* and its impact on the bibliographic description of nonbook materials. What makes *AACR2* so much better than previous codes for cataloging nonbook materials? First, and of greatest importance, one of *AACR2*'s basic principles is the equal treatment of all materials. Chapter 1 presents general rules for bibliographic description for all materials. Additional chapters address the particular characteristics of each format. Chapter 2 deals with books, while chapters 3 through 10 deal with various nonbook formats. Examples throughout the code come from books and nonbook matrials. Rules for access points address problems presented by the various formats, including the particular needs of sound recordings. For instance, films and sound recordings can be given corporate body main entry, provided the contribution of the group is more than just performance of a work.

### Effects of Automation

Beyond the impact of *AACR2* and MARC, how has automation improved the cataloging of nonbook materials? Has the inclusion of nonbook materials in bibliographic databases improved access to all materials for all users? Has standardization of bibliographic description resulted in efficient identification of materials? The major bibliographic utilities, OCLC, RLIN, and WLN, indicate that records for nonbook materials account for approximately 10 percent of their databases. In OCLC and RLIN, the number is in excess of 1 million titles. In light of the small number of school libraries (the major users of nonbook materials) participating in the utilities, this number is surprising. (It should be noted that these databases include all types of materials, not just those cataloged by the Library of Congress.)

Efforts to establish or maintain quality control in bibliographic data are exercised by network managers and participants. There has been an interesting change in the concern of library staff members for quality cataloging now that their work is visible in a national network. This newly found pride in their work has re-sulted in greater emphasis on accuracy, care in following stan-dards, and upgrading in technical knowledge. Other steps are being taken by OCLC, with the introduction of a program allowing selected libraries to correct master records, increasing the partic-ipants' responsibility for database integrity.

To develop these large databases as the core of a national union catalog of nonbook materials, we must encourage broader partic-ipation by all types of libraries. The resources of school, public, small academic, and special libraries should be added to these databases. Each library has unique materials to contribute to broad-based resource sharing. Traditionally, we thought that smaller libraries were unable to participate in the bibliographic utilities. In a 1980 article in *American Libraries*, Leon Drolet, director of the Suburban Audio Visual Service (SAVS, located in LaGrange Park, Illinois) reported that 9.2 percent of statewide film and video holdings were found in the OCLC database and that only 12.1 percent of these had Library of Congress subject head-ings.[13] In an interview, Drolet indicated that his major problem in searching rested with differing information for the same items provided by existing film lists prepared by the 18 public library systems in Illinois. Titles vary, there are few standard numbers, and there is heavy reliance on subject access, all of which made searching OCLC difficult.

The Illinois State Library's LSCA-funded Multi-Media Project, directed by Drolet, decided to develop their own integrated online system with author, title, subject, and standard number access to its records, as well as other service modules. His staff elected not to use OCLC or any other standard source of bibliographic infor-mation for the generation of their records. MARC formatting is not used. Access to these materials will be available only on a state-wide basis, or, possibly, a regional basis. Illinois libraries will be able to access the SAVS database. Should they not find the item they seek, they will have to search OCLC or another data source, thus defeating the goal of single-step searching. If librarians are faced with searching in several sources for the same item, are they not more likely to adopt the posture of not even bothering to request nonbook materials for interlibrary loan—echoing Pinion's findings?

Have the bibliographic utilities increased access to nonbook materials? Undoubtedly, yes—holding symbols identify the li-braries which own each item represented in the database. Through OCLC's integrated interlibrary loan (ILL) subsystem, materials can be requested from owning libraries via the OCLC terminal. Problems exist with varying titles for different editions or issues of an item. Improved searching techniques on the part of the requesting library, subject access, and improved cataloging by libraries entering the original data could make the utilities the resource sharing tool we seek.

**Delivering Items to Users**

For both book and nonbook materials delivery is the last barrier. Borrowing libraries filing a standard ILL form play a guessing game. Does the supplying library still own the item? Is it checked out to another patron? Is the item at the bindery or in the repair pile? Or by a stroke of luck, is the item on the shelf? Taking as long as four to six weeks, the ILL service is not satisfactory for either users or librarians. To improve turnaround time and reduce the guessing-game nature of ILL, copy information and shelf status should be attached to the bibliographic record. We realize the impracticality at this point in time of creating a national circulation system which would provide the shelf information.

How can shelf status information be provided in a manner that is both practical and realistic? I would suggest an hierarchical approach to resource sharing, beginning on the local level. This isn't a new concept; it is the same method that we have always used. However, I suggest that we begin by using local and regional automated circulation systems. Not only must access to individual circulation systems be made possible, but the databases must include information for nonbook materials. The library must do this anyway to circulate these materials using the automated system. Establishing standard data entry modes for nonbook materials following MARC and *AACR2* will provide easy access. The librarian can use the same search strategy already familiar for books. Once a particular item is located, its shelf status is also known because the bibliographic database is linked to the circulation record. We are relying on accurate and complete bibliographic information to identify the item successfully. Should the item not be available within the region, national databases can be consulted.

The second problem is associated with delivery of items in fragile nonbook formats. Typically, the last excuse for not lending nonbook materials is their fragility. Safely transporting these materials between libraries can be a problem. Films and sound recordings must be specially packed, cassettes are small and can be easily lost, microcomputer software is sensitive to heat, cold, and bending. All these materials require special care, but we should look for ways to protect the materials rather than deciding not to lend them. 16mm film cases can be used to lend sound recordings. Microcomputer software can be transferred from flimsy containers to hardcover notebooks. Users should be notified of the fragility of the materials, and materials should be insured for shipping. Whatever is necessary to ensure the care of these materials should be done; and they should be lent.

## Staff Attitudes

Without a doubt, the greatest impediment to resource sharing of nonbook materials is the negative attitude of librarians. They are still reluctant to integrate all information sources. Although today's librarian is supposed to be a link between information and the user, a major problem exists when a significant portion of the collection is excluded because the items do not fit between two pieces of cardboard. Reluctance to request nonbook materials is reinforced by the unwillingness to lend them.

Nonbook specialists must look to the principles of organization applied to books and apply them to nonbook materials. They must learn to use these principles in their operations and extend their skills to help other librarians to interact with nonbook information sources in meeting the needs of users. Gerald Brong suggests that nonbook specialists must become as competent as their book-oriented colleagues.[14] Librarians who do not routinely deal with nonbook materials should consult specialists on unfamiliar matters, including delivery and access.

We are quick to criticize the standards, MARC and *AACR2*, for their book orientations. To eliminate this bias, we must begin with book and nonbook librarians. The standards can do only so much to encourage changes which are necessary if nonbook materials are to assume a more important role in resource sharing.

Is it practical for a local library to lend nonbook materials? My experience shows that it is. A library in which I worked lent all types of materials, including videotapes, filmstrips, puzzles, games, and microcomputer software, among member libraries of the North Suburban Library System (Wheeling, Illinois), as well as in response to requests received through OCLC. Local librarians identified the owner of a requested item using a shared CLSI circulation system, placed the request electronically, and had it delivered with North Suburban's van. Over a five-year period we had no damage to any materials. Similar positive experiences resulted from lending materials to more distant partners through OCLC. Willingness to share both book and nonbook materials increased as knowledge of their availability grew. Materials were entered into a common database using standardized rules for description; staff skills were upgraded; and attempts were made to circumvent the barriers that appeared.

## Conclusion

The NCLIS study found that use of nonbook materials in networking was limited because supply and demand for them was small. Low demand does not help improve supply, and limited supply can suppress demand. It is impossible to say how demand would grow if ample supplies and really good service existed. Therein lies our challenge.

### Notes

1.   Allen Kent, "Resource Sharing in Libraries," in *Encyclopedia of Library and Information Science* (New York: Marcel Dekker, 1968), 25:294.

2.   Kent, "Resource Sharing," 295.

3.   Vernon E. Palmour et al., *Study of the Characteristics, Costs, and Magnitude of Interlibrary Loans in Academic Libraries* (Westport, Conn.: Greenwood Press, 1972).

4.   Catherine Pinion, *The Interlending and Availability of Audiovisual Materials in the United Kingdom: Report of a Survey in 1979* (Wetherby, West Yorkshire: The British Library Lending Division, 1980), 10.

5.   Gerald R. Brong, *Problems in Bibliographic Access to Nonprint Materials* (Washington D.C.: National Commission on Library and Information Science, 1979), 1.

6.   Brong, *Problems in Bibliographic Access*, 1.

7.   Brong, *Problems in Bibliographic Access*, 1.

8.   Sheila S. Intner, *Access to Media: An Investigation of Public Librarians' Bibliographic Practices and Attitudes toward Access to Nonprint Materials* (D.L.S diss., Columbia University, 1982).

9.   John Attig, "The Concept of a MARC Format," *Information Technology and Libraries* 2 (March, 1983):12.

10.   Attig, "Concept of a MARC Format," 12.

11.   Attig, "Concept of a MARC Format," 13.

12.   Attig, "Concept of a MARC Format," 13.

13.   Leon Drolet, "Illinois Libraries Share Audiovisual Materials through Pioneer Multi-media Access Project," *American Libraries* 12 (March, 1982):208.

14.   Gerald R. Brong, "The Path to Interlibrary Networking for Audiovisual Materials," in *Proceedings of the Conference on Interlibrary Communications and Information*, ed. Joseph Becker (Chicago: American Library Association, 1971), 105.

# ■ Access to Nonbook Materials: The Role of Subject Headings and Classification Numbers for Nonbook Materials

by Jean Weihs

*Traditional author-title access which serves so well for books is rarely adequate for nonbook materials. Subject analysis and classification often provide substantially greater accessibility to the rich and varied information contained in nonbook materials. Jean Weihs, a strong proponent of integrated collections, examines the subject analysis of nonbook materials.*

*In her second contribution, Weihs discusses the advantages and disadvantages of systems of subject analysis in current use in North America. She gives practical suggestions on keeping current with new terminology, which often occurs in nonbook materials long before it appears in books, the traditional source of new subject terminology. The many uses of classification, including integrated shelving and browsing demonstrate the potential benefits of greater public awareness of a library's nonbook holdings.*

At the start, I want to state my bias. I strongly believe that all records for all items in the collection of a library should be filed in one catalog. Studies have shown that most people will search only in one catalog whether they are successful in finding what they want or not.[1] Some people may be lazy, but I suspect that the majority are ignorant of the fact that there is more than one catalog. Others may not have the time to go from place to place. It is unreasonable for libraries to expect their patrons to have an in-depth knowledge of library files. The exclusion of certain materials from the main catalog may be regarded as a form of censorship if the public is not persistent in the search for information.

Another kind of censorship is to give subject headings to book materials only. I assume librarians do not need to be convinced that nonbook materials should not be excluded from the process of subject analysis, so I shall not discuss that problem. Instead,

53

let us move on to examine the subject analysis of nonbook materials.

## Problems of Subject Heading Lists and Nonbook Materials

If all records are to be filed in one catalog, the same cataloging rules must be used and the same subject heading system applied. Most North American libraries use *Sears List of Subject Headings* or *Library of Congress Subject Headings (LCSH)*. How effective are they when applied to nonbook materials? In 1976, I conducted an informal survey of 64 Canadian libraries as my contribution to the work of the American Library Association Ad Hoc Subcommittee for the Subject Analysis of Audiovisual Materials.[2] For this work, I asked some of these 64 people their opinions of the present situation. They were much less dissatisfied than they were in 1976. There have been improvements, such as far fewer book-oriented headings.

Some problems still remain.

Currency will always be a problem for all materials, but it is a greater problem for nonbook materials because new subject matter frequently appears there first. A videotape made yesterday can be on the shelves tomorrow; a book on the same topic will take much longer to produce. Standard lists of subject headings are slow to introduce new terms for these new subjects, and some librarians feel very uncomfortable about using homemade terms. *Sears* appears in new editions every few years. *LCSH* is updated more frequently by *Library of Congress Subject Headings in Microform*, and LC has recently announced the availability of its Subject Cataloging Division's internal working documents, titled *Library of Congress Subject Headings Weekly Lists*, which will make new subject headings available to catalogers some months before they are included in the microform editions. Although this is a big improvement in service, catalogers cannot expect to find a heading for every new subject because *LCSH* is developed specifically for LC collections.

Precision is also a problem. The subject content of some nonbook materials is very specific; some items deal with a single concept. Other media are not easily browsed, and they have no manuals or indexes. School librarians complain that subject heading lists do not deal with educational goals. For example, *Sears* has no headings for primary concepts, such as left and right, up and down; the heading EDUCATION, PRESCHOOL is too broad and CHILD DEVELOPMENT is not applicable. There is nothing for environmental music, for example, music that evokes a relaxing environment, or that of a jungle.

Many librarians still express unhappiness with subject headings for music. In the July 1984 issue of *Music Cataloging Bulletin*, LC published a questionnaire about subject headings for jazz and popular music. A compilation of the 125 replies, published in the January 1985 issue, revealed that slightly less than one half of the respondents found LC subject headings for jazz and popular music inadequate.[3] It is interesting that academic librarians expressed the most dissatisfaction (52.2 percent) and public librarians the least (43.2 percent). My respondents, most of whom would probably not read the *Music Cataloging Bulletin*, lined up differently—more public librarians than academic librarians were dissatisfied with *LCSH*. Public and school librarians believe the LC's classical music headings are too academic for the unsophisticated patron, and its coverage of popular music is believed to be inadequate.

Librarians who use *Sears* for their general collection seem to be more dissatisfied about music headings than *LCSH* users, because all my respondents switch to *LCSH* for these headings. Many are also unhappy about subject headings for 16mm films because of the lack of headings for genre, such as pixilation.

A new problem has arisen lately—subject headings for microcomputer software. All the people to whom I spoke and who catalog this medium mentioned this as a problem. All feel that the subject content of microcomputer software is different from that of other formats. They claim that most software has an educational objective; for example, *Lemonade* is a program in which a person must determine the price of lemonade, including a profit, when factors vary. This teaches estimating, but it is not about estimating. Similarly, software which will do word processing is not about word processing, and catalogers feel awkward doing a traditional subject analysis for these items. An analogy might be made to individual works of fiction, which are never given the heading FICTION.

Unfortunately, many of our cataloging tools do not provide cataloging for microcomputer software, so we don't have other librarians' examples to help us choose appropriate subject analysis. This will come. Some large utilities, such as UTLAS in Canada and OCLC in the United States, have implemented the MARC format for machine-readable data files. Also, LC is planning a pilot project this year to catalog 1,000 microcomputer software titles. Their experience should produce benefits beyond merely copying the 1,000 entries.

The ALA Ad Hoc Subcommittee on Subject Access to Micro-computer Software, which issued guidelines following the 1985 ALA Annual Conference, identified the following objectives to guide its recommendations:

1.  The entire record (descriptive cataloging, subject catalog-ing, and classification) should provide the access needed by the user.
2.  Sound practices of subject analysis and classification should be followed to avoid unwieldy files or useless shelf arrangements caused by grouping materials together by form alone.
3.  One must ensure that adequate subject headings and link-ages exist in *Library of Congress Subject Headings (LCSH)* and that LC classification and DDC have adequate provi-sions for the subjects covered by microcomputer software.[4]

The subcommittee believes that "the criteria for assigning sub-ject headings and classification to microcomputer software should be the same as those for the subject analysis of other works in the collection."[5]

I agree with the work of the subcommittee except on one point. The subcommittee is considering a model for subject entry which would include two subdivisions, a form subdivision and a com-puter model or operating system subdivision. I do not think the latter subdivision should be added to the catalog record. For years we have had the problem of machine-specific software; we did not give added entries or subject heading subdivisions for needed equipment when cataloging videotapes and film loops. Cataloging concepts have not changed; we have simply added a new medium. For libraries which have, or are anticipating, online catalogs, the listing of the same information twice in the record (this infor-mation appears in detail in the bibliographic description of the item, and in a MARC record it appears in both coded and uncoded form) is unnecessary and uneconomic. In any case, the need for this information may be temporary. Computer experts suggest that in the future software will become less machine-specific, with only two, or perhaps three, different systems coexisting—a situ-ation similar to videocassettes. They also predict that technolog-ical developments, such as translator disks, will obviate the need to specify necessary equipment.

There are other subject heading systems. PRECIS, which avoids inverted subject headings and subdivisions in its natural language structure, has many enthusiasts. I spoke to several people in the

Toronto area who have been involved in PRECIS-indexed catalogs. Those who have used it for nonbook materials were particularly appreciative because its depth and specificity result in an accurate description of subject content and its terminology, which is derived from the material, is current. A fairly well-known Canadian example of PRECIS indexing is the National Film Board of Canada catalog.

However, not all PRECIS pilot projects have led to its adoption. Between 1973 and 1976 the College Bibliocentre, which does the cataloging for 22 community colleges and one polytechnic institute in Ontario, assigned PRECIS to nonbook materials. Derek Robinson, who did this cataloging and found PRECIS to be an effective tool, describes the project's end:

> The response of catalog users was generally favourable, but the college librarians were inclined to prefer the devil they knew. . . . The history of PRECIS at the College Bibliocentre emphasizes the obstacles facing a new system: financial burdens, inertia, resistance to change, and North American distrust of centralization.[6]

One of the major reasons why PRECIS, despite many favorable critiques,[7] has not found wide acceptance in North America is the Library of Congress' decision not to use it.[8] In a document entitled "Freezing the Library of Congress Catalog," which was distributed at the 1978 ALA Midwinter meetings, LC listed seven conclusions resulting from their feasibility study. One of the points made and one which has recently been emphasized by Mary K. D. Pietris,[9] chief of the Subject Cataloging Division, is that "there has been no public demand that the Library of Congress either replace the traditional Library of Congress headings with PRECIS, nor to add PRECIS strings to traditional catalog cards or MARC tapes."[10] Pietris noted that LC subject catalogers liked PRECIS.[11] The waves from that decision affected MARC tapes and, consequently, both derived cataloging and shared cataloging.

Keyword access, like other subject heading systems, has problems of vocabulary control unless a library has a sophisticated automated system. Other indexes, such as *Thesaurus of ERIC Descriptors*,[12] are printed and bound and go quickly out of date if they are not constantly revised.

Susan Nesbitt, in her unpublished research project titled "Analysis of Subject Heading Lists Applied to Nonprint Materials,"[13] concluded that for a public library *Sears* is of less use than *LCSH* for nonbook materials because it is not specific enough, and

that none of the standard lists provide adequate fiction genre headings or specialized media access.

## Solutions

What are the solutions to the problems of subject headings? There
are no perfect solutions. Nevertheless, a solution, however im-
perfect, must be found in order to facilitate access to current materials. The ability to find specific topics in newer materials, many
of which are not books, is one of the reasons people come to our
libraries. Numerous studies have shown that the most heavily used
catalog search is through subject headings.[14]

Sears gives directions for the formation of subject headings not
found in its list.[15] In the *Cataloging Service Bulletin,* LC gives
directions for local expansions.[16] Some librarians use online services such as DIALOG, SDC, or BRS for clues to new subject matter,
but it is not always possible for catalogers to have access to these.
Medical librarians have a particular difficulty with currency because nonbook materials about new diseases or methods of treatment appear very quickly in medical libraries and such information is wanted immediately by medical staff. They often use
Medline to see if an item about the new subject matter has appeared.

The best and least expensive solution, in my opinion, is to
purchase the *Cataloging Service Bulletin* and the *Hennepin
County Library Cumulative Authority List*[17] and search them for
new headings. I am impressed with the research which Hennepin
County devotes to the establishment of each new heading. It is far
cheaper to buy this list than to do the work over again in your
library. If you do not have all the reference books they search, you
must buy them, and staff time used in searching is costly. (Author's
note: I want to stress the fact that I am not their agent and do not
get a commission.) The complete *Hennepin County Library Cumulative Authority List* is produced quarterly on microfiche and
costs $30 per year. Hennepin County Library also issues a bi-
monthly accumulation of new subject headings, replacement
headings, new notes, and cross references in a less-expensive print
version, titled *Hennepin County Cataloging Bulletin.* It is interesting to note that both Barbara Westby, editor of *Sears List of
Subject Headings,* and the LC Subject Cataloging Division staff
check the Hennepin County list as part of their research and sometimes use the Hennepin County headings.

The use of media form subdivisions depends on a library's

policy about subject access because the subdivisions are optional. The advantages to their use are:

1.  In a long sequence of items with the same subject heading, items in a particular format are not readily noticed. If the library wants attention brought to various formats of a heavily covered topic, media form divisions should be used.
2.  In a library where most requests link subject matter to format, the linkage is immediately obvious.

The disadvantages of media form subdivisions are:

1.  They segregate items into format groupings and thus work against the concept of a multimedia collection which promotes the idea that information comes in all forms, the information being more important than the format.
2.  The use of a general material designation and a media form subdivision results in the same term being used twice. This increases costs and is unnecessary in an automated system.

Librarians have recently expressed concern about cataloging items which are designed to hold a large number of works on a single item, such as microcomputer software and videodiscs. This is not really a new problem because we have had to deal with this in the past with large kits, microform sets, books compiled of many plays, poems, or stories, and sound recordings of many works of music. The problem relates to both descriptive cataloging and subject analysis. It is arbitrarily included in this discussion rather than in my discussion of descriptive cataloging rules. The solutions are found in *AACR2*, which provides three alternatives:

1.  Catalog each work separately and link each to the first work on the item by means of a *with* note. Each work could then have its own set of subject headings.
2.  Make author, title, and subject analytics for each work.
3.  Add name and title added entries to the tracing. Subject added entries for each work are not effective here.

The cataloger should assess the patrons' needs to determine which solution is best.

## Classification and Nonbook Materials

To begin this discussion of classification, I want to state another bias. I believe that the same classification scheme should be used for all materials. Classification is both a location and a browsing device very suitable for open access libraries, while accession numbers have a location function only and are more suited to closed access shelving. Once again, library policy will determine the suitability of either system.

My bias for classification numbers is matched to my enthusiasm for having all materials, or as many as practical, on open access. I am particularly interested in the concept of intershelving because studies have shown that the circulation of all materials, books as well as nonbook materials, rises when materials with the same subject matter are housed on the same shelves. I have written a book, *Accessible Storage of Nonbook Materials*,[18] which explores the possibility of intershelving and partial intershelving.

Even if all materials with the same classification numbers are not housed together, the classification number helps patrons to identify items on the same topic; the number emphasizes sameness. A school librarian told me the following story, which dramatizes this point. The nonbook materials in her library were kept on shelves attached to a side wall on open access, but uncataloged and unclassified. They were hardly ever used. An opportunity for extra help allowed her to have the items cataloged and classified and then returned to the same shelves as before. Suddenly, the nonbook materials began to circulate. She watched the students carefully and observed that they only used the catalog to find a Dewey number and then went to the shelves to find items with that number. This action now included nonbook materials.

Classification numbers can also be used to produce bibliographies in some automated systems. They are also used to organize collection evaluation data, to aid in the selection process, and to perform other collection management purposes. Automated circulation systems often track items by class number or broad subject areas to determine the parts of the collection that are used.

The problems associated with classification schemes are the same as those associated with subject headings, that is, currency and precision. The *Dewey Decimal Classification and Relative Index* updates itself in the publication titled *DC&: Dewey Decimal Classification Additions, Notes and Decisions*.[19] Unfortunately, this publication does not appear with great frequency. Separate schedules which need updating, such as 301–307, and schedules of proposed revisions, such as the 780s, have also been published.

Despite all this updating, the majority of libraries do not use them.

One I hope will be used is a schedule recently published dealing with computer science.[20] It includes a revision of 004–006, parts of 384.3 and 621.39, and an expansion of the subdivision –0285.

LC classification schedules are published periodically, but editions can be and often are years apart. LC offers additions and changes to the schedules in quarterly microfiches, as well as guidance in *Cataloging Service Bulletin*.

The people involved in my 1976 study to whom I spoke more recently found the updating of classification schedules more of a problem than that of subject heading systems and they were less aware of updating mechanisms.

How will automation affect subject analysis? More and more libraries will have automated authority files. It is now possible to buy the automated authority files of some national libraries. This will give libraries the ability to change subject headings by a single transaction. Changing terminology will no longer be a problem. In a sophisticated program, cross references can be built in and, combined with Boolean searching capacity, the need for standard subject heading lists may vanish.

Changing classification numbers will be more troublesome. Catalog records can be changed easily with a single keyboard transaction, but there will always be the tedious work of changing the labels of the items themselves and other things associated with circulation procedures. Shifting materials physically to their new locations is another problem that computers do not address. However, changing terminology is probably more important than changing classification numbers because out-of-date terminology may affect the patrons' view of the library and/or prevent them from getting the information wanted. Classification as applied in most libraries offers one dimension of subject access, but is not geared to register multiple topics, interdisciplinary subject matter, or other multi-dimensional subject access.

It is important to remember that technical services is really a part of public services, that the whole library should function as a public service department. Effective cataloging has as much to do with public service as reference work. This community of purpose is emphasized when all staff works in both technical and public departments for at least a few hours a week. If one catalogs nonbook materials—indeed, all materials—from the patron's point of view, the library will have a dynamic catalog.

## Conclusions

In closing, I wish to touch upon an issue that is ancillary to either descriptive cataloging or subject analysis. The Library Association of Australia Audiovisual Services Committee has recently produced *Guidelines for Packaging Nonbook Materials.*[21] This pamphlet is directed toward the producers of nonbook materials to assist them in marketing materials which are well labelled and suitably packaged for library use. The Association of American Medical Colleges in collaboration with the National Library of Medicine has also developed guidelines, titled "Attributes of Quality in Audiovisual Materials for Health Professions Education."[22] These guidelines discuss subject content and are less specific about packaging than the Australian publication. If these documents were to be circulated among North American producers and those producers were persuaded to use them, the economic benefits to libraries would be significant. For one thing, cataloging and processing would be less time-consuming; for another, the circulating life of nonbook materials would increase. Some purveyors of library products have devised ingenious methods of repackaging nonbook materials to help make them easier to shelve in booklike stacks, as well as to transport for use outside the library. Repackaging, however, is costly and time-consuming and so a less attractive alternative.

Subject cataloging and classification provide for books—the bulk of materials in the library—the chief means of obtaining wanted information. Patrons rely on lookups in the subject catalog as well as browsing along the shelves in order to find desired materials, particularly if the topic is a new or unfamiliar one. Nonbook materials are sometimes the only source of this information; at other times, they enrich and enhance the information offered by traditional print materials. Libraries can take better advantage of their nonbook dollars when they furnish the same kind of subject access for nonbook as book materials. Patrons benefit, too, by having a rich variety of resources from which to choose those that best meet their intellectual and recreational needs.

### Notes

1. Some examples of such statements are found in: Margaret M. Beckman, "Online Catalogs and Library Users," *Library Journal*, 107(Nov. 1, 1980):2044; Alan Meyer, "Some Important Findings in Catalog Use Studies," in *The Measurement and Evaluation of Library Services*, ed. F. W. Lancaster (Washington, D. C.: Information Resources Press, 1977), 70.

2.  Jean Riddle Weihs, "Problems of Subject Analysis for Audio/Visual Materials in Canadian Libraries," *Canadian Library Journal*, 33(Oct. 1976):453, 455.

3.  Harry Price, "Results of the Questionnaire on Jazz and Popular Music," *Music Cataloging Bulletin* 16, no. 1(Jan. 1985):2-3.

4.  Joan S. Marshall, "Subject Access to Microcomputer Software," *Library Resources & Technical Services* 29(Jan./March 1985):68.

5.  Marshall, "Subject Access to Microcomputer Software," 69.

6.  C. Derek Robinson, "PRECIS Canada: Achievements and Prospects," *Canadian Journal of Information Science* 4(May 1979):108.

7.  Some examples of favorable critiques: Brian Burnham and Audrey Taylor, *PRECIS Indexing: Development of a Working Model for a School Library/Information Retrieval Network* (Toronto: Ontario Ministry of Education and Ministry of Colleges and Universities, 1982); Phyllis A. Richmond, "PRECIS Compared with Other Indexing Systems," in *The PRECIS Index System: Principles, Applications, and Prospects; Proceedings of the International PRECIS Workshop . . .*, ed. Hans H. Wellisch (New York: H. W. Wilson, 1977), 101–114; Ann H. Schabas, "Postcoordinate Retrieval: A Comparison of Two Indexing Languages," *Journal of the American Society for Information Science* 33(Jan. 1982):32-37.

8.  Mary Dykstra, "The Lion That Squeaked," *Library Journal* 103(Sept. 1, 1978):1570–1572.

9.  Mary K. D. Pietris, private conversation, 20 Jan. 1986.

10.  "Freezing the Library of Congress Catalog" (Document distributed at the American Library Association Midwinter Meeting, 1978), 5.

11.  Mary K. D. Pietris, private conversation, 20 Jan. 1986.

12.  *Thesaurus of ERIC Descriptors*, 10th ed. (Phoenix: Oryx Press, 1984).

13.  Susan Nesbitt, "Analysis of Subject Heading Lists Applied to Nonprint Materials" (Master's thesis, University of Minnesota, 1983).

14.  Some examples of such statements are found in: *Online Catalogs: Requirements, Characteristics, and Costs; Report of a Conference Sponsored by the Council on Library Resources . . .*, ed. Davis B. McCard (Washington, D.C.: CLR, 1983), 20; Audrey Taylor, "But I Have Promises to Keep—PRECIS, an Alternative for Subject Access," in *Subject Cataloging: Critiques and Innovations*, ed. Sanford Berman (New York: Haworth Press, 1984), 82.

15.  *Sears List of Subject Headings*, 12th ed., ed. Barbara Westby (New York: H. W. Wilson, 1982), 24.

16.  *Cataloging Service Bulletin* 16:(Spring 1982)52-67.

17.  *Hennepin County Library Cumulative Authority List* (Minnetonka, Minn.: Hennepin County Library, quarterly, microfiche).

18.  Jean Weihs, *Accessible Storage of Nonbook Materials* (Phoenix, Ariz.: Oryx Press, 1984). The bibliography lists many books and articles attesting to the success of intershelving.

19.  *DC&: Dewey Decimal Classification Additions, Notes and Decisions* (Albany, N.Y.: Forest Press, irregular).

20.  *DDC/Dewey Decimal Classification. 004–006 Data Processing and Computer Science and Changes in Related Disciplines: Revision of Edition 19*, prepared by Julianne Beall (Albany, N.Y.: Forest Press, 1985).

21.  Library Association of Australia, Audiovisual Services Committee, *Guidelines for Packaging Nonbook Materials* (Sydney: LAA, 1984).

22.  "Attributes of Quality in Audiovisual Materials for Health Professions Education," *Journal of Biocommunication* 8, no. 2(July 1981):6–11.

■

# ■ Authority Control and System Design

by Arlene G. Taylor

The results of authority control processes are critical in all catalogs because they constitute the interface between the user seeking information and the objects in the collection which contain that information. Arlene G. Taylor, a leading expert in authority control and a participant in RTSD's successful Authority Control Institutes, shows how authority control for nonbook materials is carried out in the same way as for book materials.

In this work (which was first presented before the Music Library Association's 1985 Preconference on Authority Control) Taylor discusses authority control in the online environment, first describing features of existing authority systems and then reporting on the efficacy of a particular system in a nonbook environment. She presents two principles of authority control: (1) ensuring that a user will find all manifestations of a name under one form; and (2) providing a reference structure so that a user will find a name or title sought if the catalog has it. It is her assertion that while existing systems are adequately designed to deal with the first principle, considerable rethinking may be required to accomplish the second.

Authority control for nonbook materials is carried out in the same way as for book materials. There may be proportionately more of some types of headings for some nonbook materials (e.g., there are proportionately more uniform titles for music scores and musical sound recordings than for most other materials), but the processes and effects of authority control are the same.

For many years, we have had authority control in a manual mode. Human intervention is the only link between a manual authority file and its associated bibliographic records. Automated

Arlene G. Taylor is Assistant Professor at the Graduate Library School of the University of Chicago. She is author of Cataloging with Copy and AACR2 Headings.

authority control systems have brought some changes in this area. With automated systems there can be more than an intellectual link between an authority file and a bibliographic file. Headings in new bibliographic records can be checked automatically against the authority file to determine whether the heading is already present. If it is not, the system can signal the need for validation (i.e., the process of checking new headings against authority file headings and references to determine whether headings have already been established, and to verify spelling and content designators, if established).

In an automated system all works of an author or on a subject can be displayed together regardless of whether the name or subject term is searched in "correct" form or in a form that has been entered in the authority record as a reference. References can be generated automatically. When a heading changes, all occurrences of the heading in the bibliographic file can be changed automatically. In addition, all occurrences of the heading as a subdivision or qualifier can be changed (e.g., when ARGENTINE REPUBLIC is changed to ARGENTINA, then SANTA ROSA, ARGENTINE REPUBLIC can also be changed to SANTA ROSA (ARGENTINA) and EDUCATION—ARGENTINE REPUBLIC can be changed to EDUCATION—ARGENTINA). This kind of control was almost never achieved in manual files because of the near impossibility of finding all such headings.

The systems currently available, however, do not all offer all of the aforementioned features. There are, in general, two groups of authority control systems:

1. those that offer processing of a library's bibliographic records
2. those that offer online access to authority records.

The systems that offer processing typically process the archive tapes that a library has accumulated as it has participated in a bibliographic network. These tapes are compared by computer to authority records and are edited to change older forms of heading to newer forms, to correct MARC tagging errors, to correct spacing, to detect common spelling errors, and to detect near matches (e.g., nearly identical dates). Such processing can also be used to create a machine-readable authority record for each heading in the bibliographic file. The files resulting from such processing can be used to create COM or online catalogs.

The systems that offer online access to authority files fall into one of two groups.[1] Either the authority files are completely separate from the bibliographic files, or the authority files are linked with the bibliographic files in some way. Examples of the first type (authority and bibliographic files separate and unlinked) are OCLC and RLIN.

Networks that have more integrated authority control are UTLAS and WLN. In these two systems, texts of headings are stored only in the authority file. A sequence number for the appropriate heading is stored in the bibliographic record in a designated field. When a bibliographic record is displayed, the sequence numbers in it are replaced with appropriate text. This happens whether the search term was the "authorized" heading or one from which a see reference is made. In both cases, the "authorized" heading replaces the sequence number.

While the method of storing headings only in authority files saves space in computer files, it may also slow response time when the system must retrieve the text of one or more headings from an authority file before displaying a bibliographic record. However, another advantage of storing text only in the authority file is that any needed change is made only to the authority record. If the system stores text of headings in all records, all must be located and changed whenever a revision is necessary.

Networks, whose authority structures have just been discussed, provide their services by allowing member libraries to use a common database. Online authority control is also provided by some of the commercial vendors who are in the business of providing an individual library with its own unique catalog and authority file.

A vendor usually begins to provide online authority control by taking the library's machine-readable database through a process that results in a list of every unique heading used. After the list is edited, it is used as the basis for the library's authority file. From then on, headings from every new bibliographic record added to the system are validated against the authority file. If an exact match is found, the bibliographic record number is added to those already associated with the authority record. If there is no match, some systems create a new authority record in skeletal form with the information available from the bibliographic record. Other systems list the headings for which there are no matching authority records and refer them to the cataloger for authority work.

In some systems, a match is made when a new heading matches a see reference as well as when it matches an authorized form in an authority record. Such a practice, however, is not a good idea, particularly for personal names and to a lesser extent for series and uniform titles. There are too many cases where the form in a *see* reference can refer to more than one heading. For example, the heading MCKAY, SUSAN J. may have a reference from MCKAY, S.J. Later another work may be added to the collection by an S.J. McKay who is a different person. It would not be correct for the system automatically to change the later heading to MCKAY, SUSAN J.

A few systems provide what is called *invisible referencing* in searching. This process is related to the practice of assuming that a match to a *see* reference is a match to the heading that reference is under. In invisible referencing, the user is given bibliographic entries for the authorized heading when the form used in the search matches a *see* reference to the authorized heading. This may not be much of a problem with subject headings. The user who asks for works on MARXISM and is given works on SOCIALISM may or may not be confused. However, the user who asks for works by David St. John and is given works by the poet David St. John *and* works by Howard Hunt, who uses the pseudonym David St. John, may be quite confused. Because of this potential confusion, most linked systems use an intermediate step. A message explaining that the user's term matches a *see* reference is given. In some systems, the user must then key in the "correct" heading. In others, the user may be instructed to press the carriage return to view records under the authorized heading.

Authority files, when linked to bibliographic files, serve as indexes to the bibliographic files. Some vendors, however, provide indexes instead of authority files in order to save disk space and to improve response time. The difference between an authority file and an index is that an authority record has reference and note fields, while an index entry does not. Because of this, the index's advantage of saved space and improved response time is offset by its inability to generate references when needed. However, not all authority records need references. There is evidence that fewer than half of all personal name authority records contain references and that many of the references that exist are unnecessary in an online catalog (see discussion later in this chapter). A possible compromise is that planned for the NOTIS system (the integrated bibliographic system of the Northwestern University Library) in which authority records will be made only for headings that require references, and the index will be made up of all names and references from both the bibliographic file and the authority file.

Only some of the systems have the means for total authority

control. In one such system, DOBIS, new cataloging is input by the method of *conversational cataloging*. The system prompts for successive parts of bibliographic records. When headings are input, the system only goes to the next prompt if the heading is authorized. If it is new to the system, an authority record is created for it before going on to the next prompt. If it matches a *see* reference, the system responds with the established form. If the established form is wanted, pressing carriage return will enter it into the record. If not, a new authority record is made, distinguishing the new heading from the *see* reference on the unwanted authority record. It is also possible in some systems to search for an authority record before entering a heading. If one is found, pressing carriage return will enter the heading from the authority record, thus avoiding typographical errors.

Two of the totally integrated systems are related to the networks. LS/2000, being marketed by OCLC, is unlike OCLC in approach. While OCLC has no linkage between authority file and bibliographic file, LS/2000 provides for checking all new bibliographic records against the authority file. Although new headings are entered automatically into the system, an *audit trail* is made so that catalogers can complete authority work on new headings. When headings are revised in the authority file, they are also automatically changed everywhere they occur in the bibliographic file (called *global change*).

BLIS is a vended system based on WLN software but not marketed by WLN. When entering original cataloging, the user can give a check command, and every heading field under authority control is checked. Those headings already in the authority file are validated, while nonmatching terms are identified either as matching a *see* reference or as being completely new to the system. The cataloger can then take appropriate action.

The major advantage of a totally integrated system is the automatic transcription of headings into bibliographic records without rekeying. A disadvantage occurs when the person who enters bibliographic records must be qualified to create authority records for new headings. More terminal time is required when decisions have to be made at the terminal.

The preceding discussion has been from the point of view of the advantages of linked authority systems for the cataloger in the process of maintaining authority control when creating the catalog. It is also important to consider how useful such linkage is for the library patron who uses an online catalog.

Some have asserted that authority control is unnecessary on-

Figure 1
**Variant forms of one person's name**

> Arlene Taylor Dowell
> Arlene T. Dowell
> Arlene Dowell
> A. T. Dowell
> Arlene G. Taylor
> Arlene Taylor
> A. G. Taylor

Figure 2
**Variant forms of one corporate name**

> Wall Street Journal
> Wall Street Journal—New York
> Wall Street JNL.—NYC
> Wall St. Jnl.—NYC
> Wall Street Journal—NYC
> Wall Street Journal, NYC
> Wall Street Journal (New York)
> Wall Street Journal, N.Y.
> Wall Street Journal (N.Y.)
> Wall St. Journal
> WSJ—NYC

line because search keys and truncation capabilities bring together variant forms of a name.[2] Malinconico, however, has argued that one cannot know when to end an unsuccessful search when there is no control.[3] Consider, for example, the author shown in figure 1 who has tried to be consistent in use of name within the constraints of one necessary name change, but whose name has appeared at least once in each of these ways. Suppose there were no authority control and a user found one of the names, let's say Dowell, but not the title sought (let's say the user doesn't know the exact title) which is under Taylor. How would the user know, having found Dowell, to try alternate forms? Note that even with authority control there would be some difficulty here. At present the authority record for this name contains no references because only the first form has appeared on title pages of books. The other forms have appeared only on articles or in citations.

Consider the corporate name shown in figure 2 that was found

Table 1
**Sample Size**

|  | Music Study | Overall Study |
|---|---|---|
| Author searches No hits | 17.6% | 22.3% |
| Title searches No hits | 56.1% | 37.1% |

by Cathy Elias to have been entered into an online file at an oil company office in twenty different ways, some of which are shown here.[4] The file had been created by only three people who were quite certain they had entered all names consistently. Note that if this title were entered into a catalog, one of the forms would be chosen, but there would be few, if any, references from the other forms.

In contemplating this situation, one wonders how effective we are at assisting users in finding a form of name chosen as a catalog heading. For many personal names, the different forms are only variations in fullness, and in a system with right-hand truncation, a search for the first word plus a letter or two of the second would bring up a list from which the desired name could be chosen. How often do users search for forms of names that are not the ones chosen by catalogers as headings, and how often would those users be assisted by linked authority records with references from forms of names not chosen as headings?

To explore these questions, I worked with Jean Dickson to analyze data from a transaction log tape of user searches in the online public catalog of NOTIS. We analyzed author and title searches made in January 1983 that had resulted in zero hits. The reports of our original studies were published in *Cataloging & Classification Quarterly*, Spring 1984.[5]

To isolate some data that would be specifically related to nonbook materials, I pulled from the original data those searches made from terminals in the Music Library at Northwestern. At the Music Library at Northwestern there are greater numbers of "nonbooks" than books. I have compared the findings from the study of music library searches with the findings of the overall study, and all examples given here are from the Music Library.[6]

In the overall study, the number of author searches that resulted in no hits represented 22.3 percent of all author searches made (see table 1). In the Music Library, the no-hit author searches

Table 2
**Author Searches Bound to Fail**

|  | Music Study | Overall Study |
|---|---|---|
| Forename first | 20.4% | 16.7% |
| e.g., A = IVAN GALAMIAN | | |
| Typos; obvious mistakes | 13.0% | 5.7% |
| e.g., A = HANDEL, GELRGE F | | |
| Attempt at Boolean search | 7.4% | 4.1% |
| e.g., A = BACH JOHANN + TRIO | | |
| Wrong file | 5.6% | 5.7% |
| e.g., A = BRASS INSTRUMENTS | | |
| Exact repeat of preceding failed search | 3.7% | 3.4% |
| e.g., A = HANDEL G F | | |
| A = HANDEL G F | | |

represented 17.6 percent of all author searches made. No-hit title searches represented 37.1 percent of all the searches overall, but 56.1 percent of all title searches in the Music Library. Music users seem to be better than average at finding authors, but not so good at finding titles. The numbers of searches here are quite small, this being a sample of a sample. There were 54 no-hit author searches in a total of 307 author searches, and 88 no-hit title searches in a total of 157 title searches. The fact that there were twice as many author as title searches in the music sample is interesting, because in the overall study there were slightly more title searches than author searches. In any case, because this is a small sample, the percentages shown must not be taken too literally.

Tables 2 through 5 give data relating to no-hit author searches. A number of the zero hits resulted from users inputting searches that were bound to fail. Table 2 gives a breakdown of these searches. There is no way that linked authority records could have helped the user in these searches. The NOTIS system did not, at the time, have the capability of inverting a name when the user input a forename before a surname. If the system were programmed to search for GALAMIAN, IVAN after a search for IVAN GALAMIAN failed, a hit would have resulted. In some systems (e.g., MELVYL) users can input a personal name in any order, and the system will search for all headings that contain the discrete words of the search.

Typographical errors are the second most frequent group

shown in table 2. These cannot, for the most part, be anticipated by either authority file references or system programming. The third category is Boolean searches. NOTIS cannot handle Boolean searches. Some of the Boolean-like searches would have been helped, however, by a system program to search the first word of the search argument followed by the first letter of the next word. This is discussed in more detail with the next table.

The fourth category is for "wrong file." Entry of a title or subject after A = will, of course, invoke the author index rather than the title or subject indexes. A user's repetition of a preceding failed search (the last category in table 2) is an interesting phenomenon. It appears that the user is thinking, "Computer, you must not have been listening the first time. Now *listen* to me *this* time."

After eliminating the "bound to fail" searches, I looked for authority records for the remaining names, and also searched NOTIS for them myself. They fell into the categories shown in table 3. The NOTIS system has automatic right-hand truncation and also ignores punctuation. Therefore, if, as in the first category, the user input REICHE EU and if NOTIS had something under REICHE, EUGEN, a match would be made.

Beginning with the second category in table 3, each category is subdivided according to whether having the authority file linked to the bibliographic file would have assisted the user in finding the name that was probably being sought. To make this distinction, I searched in OCLC and in the Library of Congress' MUMS file for LC authority records. If one was found, I checked whether or not it contained a reference from the form input by the user. If only a bibliographic record, and not an authority record, was found, I judged on the basis of my knowledge of rules and LC practice whether a reference would be made upon creation of an authority record for that name.

In the second category in table 3, a misspelled word was one that was identified after finding a correct form in NOTIS, OCLC, RLIN, or MUMS (LC). (The obvious misspellings were counted under "Typos: Obvious Mistakes" in table 2.) Many of the misspellings are the result of the existence of common variants in the spelling of many forenames and surnames. For examples of these, see figure 3.

In the overall study, of the 151 misspellings in table 3, 117 occurred in the first word, while 34 occurred in the second or a later word. With automatic right-hand truncation, it might be possible to program the system to search for the first word plus the first letter of the second word if the search for the fuller name

Table 3
**Other Problem Author Searches**

|  | Music Study | Overall Study |
|---|---|---|
| 1) Perfectly good name, but not in NOTIS,<br>e.g.,<br>user: A = REICHE EU<br>LCAF: Reiche, Eugen | 18.5% | 22.4% |
| 2) Misspelled word | 18.5% | 22.1% |
|   a. authority record would have helped<br>    user: A = GOLDMARK KARL<br>    LCAF: Goldmark, Carl<br>       x Goldmark, Karl | 1 | |
|   b. authority record would not have helped<br>    user: A = SHOSTAKOVITCH, DIMITRI<br>    LCAF: Shostakovich, Dmitrii | 9 | |
| 3) Middle initial stops truncation | 5.6% | 5.6% |
|   a. authority record would have helped<br>    user: A = CHESHIRE, D F<br>    LCAF: Cheshire, David F.<br>       x Cheshire, D. F. | 2 | |
|   b. authority record would not have helped<br>    user: A = HANDEL G F<br>    LCAF: Handel, George Frideric | 1 | |
| 4) Incorrect spacing | 3.7% | 2.2% |
|   b. authority record would not have helped<br>    user: A = SAINTFOIX, GEORGES DE<br>    LCAF: Saint Foix, Georges de<br>    user: A = BACH, JS | 2 | |
| 5) Too much of name put in | 3.7% | 1.6% |
|   b. authority record would not have helped<br>    user: A = GABBARD, GLEN O. MD<br>    LCAF: Gabbard, Glen O. | 2 | |
| 6) Other<br>e.g., forenames in wrong order; initial words not complete; couldn't find | | 10.3% |

fails. A similar feature is available in searching names in RLIN, where the first initial after the surname can appear as the initial of *any* forename (not just the first) and will produce a match. (This

---

Figure 3
**Variant spellings of names**

| User Input | Name Found |
|---|---|
| Brubacker, Gwen | Brubaker, Gwendolyn |
| Handel George Frederick | Handel, George Frideric |
| Issarlo | Isarlo, George |
| Murato, Margaret | Murata, Margaret |

---

feature is sometimes referred to in information retrieval literature as *fuzzy matching*.)

It is also possible to consider coding names with sound-based codes such as those used by various airlines. In such a system, IVERSEN and IVERSON can both be retrieved if either is input. The same would be true of MCLEAN and MACLEAN. A paper on this subject by Karen Roughton and David Tyckoson was given at the 1985 Midwinter Meeting of ALA.[7]

Referring again to table 3, the third category consists of names where the user put in a second forename initial after a first forename initial, but because the authorized heading gives the first forename in full, there could be no match. With automatic right-hand truncation, the user would get a hit with CHESHIRE, D. but not with CHESHIRE, D.F. Authority records only include references from the surname followed by forename initials if the author has used that form on an item for which a bibliographic record has been made. But authors are *cited* that way whether or not they have ever *written* that way. Here again is a place to consider programming the system to search for the first work plus the first letter that follows.

In the fourth category of table 3, there were several instances where the user did not leave a space that should have been there, as in the second example. In this case, leaving the space would not have produced a hit, although in some cases it would have (e.g., ELIOT, T.S., instead of ELIOT, TS). But this is another place in which a program to search the first word plus the next letter input would be useful.

The fifth category in table 3 is another that would be assisted by a program to search for the first word plus the first letter that follows. All items in this category would have been found.

The "Other" category is shown on table 3 to account for the remaining searches in the overall study. None of these types were represented in the sample from the Music Library.

Table 4
**Cross References Found in Authority Records**

|  | Number of Authority Records | Percent of Total |
|---|---|---|
| Contained no x-refs | 138 | 57.5% |
| Contained only x-refs that varied in forename fullness | 35 | 14.6% |
| Contained only x-refs with spelling variations | 23 | 9.6% |
| Contained x-refs from variant forms other than fullness or spelling | 44 | 18.3% |
| | Grossman, Allen R. x Grossman, Allen | |

One last finding is worth noting even though it cannot be considered statistically valid in any way. In the process of searching for the 438 names from the overall study represented in table 3, LC authority records were found for 240 names. Although these do not represent a random sample of authority records, I noticed that many had no cross references. Table 4 shows that 57.5 percent contained no references. While the remaining 42.5 percent did contain references, few of them used forms of name chosen by the users in this study. References from forms of the name in which forenames varied in fullness were contained in 14.6 percent of the records. Several of these took the form of the example shown at the bottom of table 4. Such a reference is unnecessary in a system with automatic right-hand truncation.

Almost all references from variations in fullness of forenames would be rendered unnecessary if the system were programmed to search zero hits by the first word plus the first letter of the second. References from forms of the name with variations in the spelling of one or more words (almost always including the first word of the heading) were contained in 9.6 percent of the records. Most of these represented variant transliterations of non-Roman alphabet names. The remaining 18.3 percent contained references from variations other than spelling or fullness (some of those records also included variant spelling and/or fullness references). Examples in the last category were pseudonyms and earlier names used by authors.

Table 5 is a summary of the findings on author searches. For 5.6 percent of the Music Library searches (6.4 percent of the overall

Table 5
**Summary**

|  | Music Study | Overall Study |
|---|---|---|
| Categories 2–6 of table 3 | | |
| Of these: | | |
| Authority records would have helped | 5.6% | 6.4% |
| Authority records would not have helped | 25.9% | 38.6% |
| A right truncation program would have helped | 11.1% | 16.6% |
| Authority records could not have helped (total from table 2) | 50.0% | 46.1% |
| Of these: | | |
| A flip program would have helped | 20.4% | 21.6% |
| A right truncation program would have helped | 9.3% | 1.7% |

study), either an authority record exists that carries it in a reference from the form input by the user, or I judged that such a reference would be made were the record created. For 25.9 percent of the searches, no such reference would be made. For 50 percent of the searches, authority records, by their rules and nature, could not have helped had they been linked.

Two systems programs would have provided more assistance. A program to "flip" order of names would have helped 20.4 percent of the time, and a program to search the first word plus the first letter of the second word would also have helped in 20.4 percent (11.1 percent and 9.3 percent) of the searches in the Music Library.

I looked also at zero-hit title searches from the Music Library terminal because I wondered if users would search for forms of titles that would appear as references on authority records for uniform titles. I found only two such searches. Table 6 shows the kinds of zero-hit searches found. These, unfortunately, cannot be compared with data from the overall study, with the exception of the percentage of titles beginning with initial articles. Titles in the overall study were analyzed by Jean Dickson, who used different categories because she was asking different questions of the data.

The highest percentage of zero-hit searches was for perfectly good titles that were not in the system. Falling close to the same percentage were title searches that included initial articles. These

Table 6
**Failed Title Searches**

|  | Music Study |
|---|---|
| OK, not in NOTIS | 20.5% |
| Initial article included | 19.3% |
|    user: T = A HISTORY OF WESTERN MUSIC | |
| Word(s) wrong | 11.4% |
|    x-ref in LCAF: | |
|      user: T = PSAUTIER HUGUENOT | |
|      LCAF: Genevan psalter | |
|          x Psautier Huguenot | |
|    no x-ref: | |
|      user: T = HARMONIC ANALYSIS IN TONAL MUSIC | |
|      Bib.: Harmonic materials in tonal music | |
| Wrong file | 11.4% |
|    user: T = UMMEL B | |
|        T = SEX—THERAPY | |
| Typo or misspelling | 10.2% |
|    user: T = OPERA ASDRAMA | |
|    Bib.: Opera as drama | |
| Words left out | 6.8% |
|    user: T = HANDBOOK TO PIANOFORTE WORKS OF JOHANNES BRAHMS | |
|    Bib.: Handbook to the pianoforte works of Johannes Brahms | |
| Boolean search or statement of responsibility included | 6.8% |
|    user: T = COLLECTED WORKS OF CPE BACH | |
|        T = VARIETY = A = REGER, MAX | |
| Other | 9.1% |
|    e.g., exact repeat; extra words included; subtitle included | |
| Don't know | 4.5% |
|    user: T = EIGHT STARS ON A | |

searches represented 16 percent of the overall sample. (Only two of the Music Library users recognized the problem and repeated the search without the article.) It should be possible to write a program that would eliminate initial articles for users.

The next category in table 6, "Word(s) Wrong," is the one I thought might be assisted by linked authority records, but only two searches would have been helped. Eight searches were like the second example—a result of not remembering correctly.

Figure 4
**One user's search sequence**

    a = Bach, J. S.    [no hits]
    requests help screen
    a = Johann    [138 hits]
    a = Johann S Bach    [no hits]
    a = Johann    [138 hits]
    s = string trio    [13 subject terms]
    [browses hits]
    a = J S Bach    [no hits]
    a = Bach    [717 hits]
    a = Bach Johann    [423 hits]
    [browses #65-69]
    a = Bach Johann + Trio    [no hits]
    a = Bach Johann    t = trio    [no hits]
    a = Bach Johann    [423 hits]
    a = Bach Johann Sebastian    [358 hits]
    [browses for 8 minutes]
    s = string trio    [13 subject terms]
    [looks at line 3 again]
    [11 minutes pass before next search]

Searches in the wrong file represented 11.4 percent of the no-hit title searches. (Only two of these users recognized the error and corrected the command.) One may note that the second example is not particularly music related. It seems that musicians are human beings, too.

As expected, there were several typographical errors or misspellings. The example in the table 6 category "Words Left Out," in this case *the*, is interesting to speculate about. Did the user "learn" in an earlier search, where an initial article had been used, that articles should be dropped?

The first example under the next category in table 6 also illustrates an interesting problem. The phrase "of Johannes Brahms" is part of the title proper in the preceding example; but I could not find any titles proper that included "of C.P.E. Bach." How is a user to know when such a statement is part of a title proper?

The "Other" category in table 6 includes titles with extra words and titles that included subtitles. The last category includes titles that I could not identify although they appear to be plausible titles.

Also of interest, I looked at what the Music Library users did next after a search failed. Figure 4 illustrates a sequence of steps

Table 7
**Next Search After No Hit**

| | Author | Title | Total | |
|---|---|---|---|---|
| Unsuccessful | 27.8% | 27.3% | 27.5% | |
| Successful | 24.1% | 27.3% | 26.1% | |
| Gave up | 24.1% | 21.6% | 22.5% | [note: gave up & new |
| Help screen | 16.7% | 11.4% | 13.4% | search = 33.1%] |
| New search | 7.4% | 12.5% | 10.6% | |

Table 8
**Next Search After Unsuccessful Search or Request for Help Screen**

| | Author | Title | Total | |
|---|---|---|---|---|
| Unsuccessful | 11.1% | 15.9% | 14.1% | |
| Successful | 9.3% | 8.0% | 8.5% | |
| Gave up | 16.7% | 6.8% | 10.6% | [note: gave up & new |
| Help screen | 1.9% | 1.1% | 1.4% | search = 16.9%] |
| New search | 5.6% | 6.8% | 6.3 | |

obviously made by the same user. Table 7 summarizes the immediate next step taken after a no-hit search. I judged the next step successful if the search was related to the no-hit search in some way and if it made a hit. It was unsuccessful if it was related to the no-hit search and did not result in a hit. I judged that someone gave up if two minutes passed and the next search was unrelated. "New Search" means less than two minutes passed and the next search was unrelated. These searches may or may not have been conducted by the same person. Thirty-three percent either gave up or started a new search.

Table 8 summarizes the next step taken by users who, in table 7, were shown as either unsuccessful or who requested a help screen. Another 17 percent dropped out here. (Table 8 percentages are given in terms of the original no-hit searches.)

It can be seen in table 9 that after two or more tries after a no-hit search, half had given up, just over a third had made a successful search, and 16 percent were still trying. If half the users who get no hits give up after two tries, and if only five or six percent would have been helped by linked authority files, it seems obvious that we must work on improving reference structure and system design to aid these users.

Table 9
**After Two More Tries After No Hit**

| | |
|---|---|
| Successful | 34.6% |
| Gave up or started new search | 50.0% |
| Persisting | 15.5% |

Two principles of authority control have been separated in the preceding discussion. The first principle is that aspect of authority control that ensures that a user will find all manifestations of a name under one form. It has been shown by careful argument and by research that this principle is essential to successful searching. Users must be confident that once they have found a name, they will find everything relating to that person or body there, or they will be referred to other related material. Otherwise, users could never know when to stop searching for variant forms. This part of authority control requires that a human or machine determine, during the cataloging process, whether a heading is already present in the system, either in its current form or in a variant form. While such control is essential, it may be possible to achieve without creating an elaborate MARC-formatted authority record with all its fixed fields, subfields, etc., for every name. It may be that index entries, as planned for the NOTIS system mentioned earlier, could serve as well.

The second principle of authority control is the aspect that provides a reference structure so that a user will find a name or title sought if the catalog has it. The assumption has been that references must be provided only from variant forms of names that have appeared prominently in published works (excluding analytic parts of those works). However, if users in other libraries search in similar ways to the searches from Northwestern analyzed in this study, it would appear that linked authority records will not be sufficient and that some computer programs could provide much more assistance.

It is my belief that the authority control we have developed has been designed to assist with the first principle, but not with the second. To be of assistance with the second principle, we need to rethink the rules for references, to consider what kinds of authority records will be of benefit to users, and to investigate system designs that will be more forgiving when users fail to outguess the forms of entry we have chosen for our catalogs.

# Notes

1. For a more detailed description of these systems see: Arlene G. Taylor, Margaret F. Maxwell, and Carolyn O. Frost, "Network and Vendor Authority Systems," *Library Resources & Technical Services* 29(April/June 1985):195–205.

2. Frederick G. Kilgour, "Design of Online Catalogs," in *The Nature and Future of the Catalog* (Phoenix, Ariz.: Oryx Press, 1979), 37–38; Hugh C. Atkinson, "The Electronic Catalog," in *The Nature and Future of the Catalog*, 103–104.

3. S. Michael Malinconico, "Bibliographic Data Base Organization and Authority File Control," in *Authority Control: The Key to Tomorrow's Catalog* (Phoenix, Ariz.: Oryx Press, 1982), 1–18.

4. Cathy Ann Elias, "Authority Control in a Communication System at Standard Oil (Indiana)" (Master's thesis, Graduate Library School, University of Chicago, 1982).

5. Jean Dickson, "An Analysis of User Errors in Searching an Online Catalog," *Cataloging & Classification Quarterly* 4(Spring 1984):19–38; Arlene G. Taylor, "Authority Files in Online Catalogs: An Investigation of Their Value," *Cataloging & Classification Quarterly* 4(Spring 1984):1–17.

6. These data were originally presented at the Music Library Association Preconference on Authority Control, Louisville, Kentucky, March 5, 1985.

7. Karen G. Roughton and David A. Tyckoson, "Browsing with Sound: Sound-based Codes and Automated Authority Control," *Information Technology and Libraries* 4(June 1985):130–136.

■

# ■ Nonbook Materials in the Online Public Access Catalog

by Carolyn O. Frost

*In this chapter, Carolyn O. Frost explores the implications of online public access catalogs (OPACs) for access to information about items in nonbook formats. First, she furnishes details about the capabilities of current OPACs. This description is followed by close examination of emerging technologies and their special significance for nonbook materials.*

*In the automated library of the future, catalogs that can display visual and aural data could supplement textual bibliographic data, offering catalog users much more vivid images of the documents they represent. The old adage, "One picture is worth a thousand words," would take on a new meaning for information storage and retrieval systems.*

*Frost's thoughtful analysis of improvements that already have been implemented in present-day catalogs highlights those areas in which traditional modes of access fail to fully describe items in nonbook formats. Should the future developments projected here become a reality, the service potential of the catalog would seem to extend as far beyond today's limits as we have progressed since the wall catalogs of ancient days.*

The online public access catalog (OPAC) as we currently know it is radically changing the way in which catalogs provide access to materials in libraries' collections. What are the major capabilities of current OPACs? Which ones will have a significant impact on the kinds of access provided for nonbook materials? These and related questions will be addressed in the first part of this paper.

Carolyn O. Frost is Associate Professor at the School of Information and Library Science of the University of Michigan, Ann Arbor, and author of *Cataloging Nonbook Materials: Problems in Theory and Practice.*

What kinds of access to nonbook materials might be provided in the foreseeable future? What emerging technologies point to even more radically different modes of retrieval and description? The second part of this paper will explore possibilities for future use of online technologies which have special significance for nonbook materials.

These questions will be examined in light of qualities considered unique to nonbook materials. Also covered will be the idea that key differences and similarities between nonbook materials and print media have helped determine the way in which records for nonbook materials are retrieved and described.

Three stages can be identified as central in the development of present and future OPACs. First, there was a stage in which unique qualities of nonbook materials posed obstacles to their integration into single, multimedia catalogs and databases. Second, there was an era marked by developments in the standardization of bibliographic description, an era which helped make integration possible by recognizing attributes common to all formats. Through their inclusion in integrated machine-readable databases, nonbook materials have shared the benefits of computerized access in ways similar to books. This chapter will take special note of the attributes of nonbook materials which have benefited in particular from present capabilities of OPACs.

Emerging technologies suggest a third stage. While current utilization of OPACs for nonbook materials has taken place in an integrated environment which presupposes common characteristics of media and standardization, future technologies point to separate, specialized systems. These specialized systems would recognize the unique qualities of nonbook formats and provide modes of access and description which relate directly to these qualities, allowing the media to communicate, as it were, in their own language. Such technologies would allow the user to query the access system in methods which are outside the traditional verbal, printed access points and description elements.

Prototypes of some such systems are already under development, while others are strictly in the idea stage, but within the realm of technical feasibility. These can be viewed as adjunct systems which would supplement, rather than supplant, current integrated catalogs. As adjunct systems, they could extend the present catalog. In both present and future systems, there is the potential for new kinds of access to and description of nonbook materials.

**Current Capabilities**

This section will examine two types of generic capabilities of OPACs. (Given the range of systems and options available, no one system is presented in this discussion; instead, we have in mind a composite of the capabilities from various systems now in use which have been demonstrated as feasible.) Some generic capabilities of OPACs enhance access equally for both nonbook materials and books. The ability to search the holdings of a collection at one terminal, multiple terminal sites, remote access, immediate interactive communication between user and system, the ability to update information online, are some of the capabilities which enrich and extend the quality of access to all materials.

Developments in the standardization of bibliographic description, such as AACR2, and in the standardization of machine-readable formats, such as MARC, have enabled nonbook materials to be included in databases of the major bibliographic utilities as well as in other machine-readable databases. Such advances in standardization have helped resolve problems posed by diverse standards which emphasized the ways in which nonbook materials differ from books, rather than acknowledging their commonality. Attributes common to all media have served as the basis for a standard framework of description. While such systems for standardization are still far from perfect, they have provided an essential starting point.

With the progress of bibliographic standardization and the integration of nonbook materials into databases from which local OPACs can be derived, nonbook formats have shared the benefits of online access capabilities. Of special interest to us are those generic capabilities which benefit all formats, but have a particular impact on nonbook materials, and which have the potential for resolving some key problems in description and access. These problems derive from attributes of nonbook materials which differ substantially from print formats; attributes which, in the opinions of some, have diminished the value of standardized systems. We will consider ways in which these problems have been addressed by the following capabilities of OPACs:

1. expanding the number and kinds of access points
2. combining access points
3. access by classification notation
4. access by keyword, and by truncated form of a search term.

The first two capabilities will be considered together.

*Expanding the Number and Kinds of Access Points*
Online public access catalogs provide the potential for increasing the number and kinds of access points by which nonbook materials can be made accessible to searchers. Depending on the system design, almost any field of the bibliographic record can be used as an access point. Whereas in manual systems the primary points of access have been author, title, and subject heading, the capability for providing access to many different fields allows us to exploit a great deal more of the information contained in bibliographic records used to describe nonbook materials.

*Combining Access Points*
Online search capabilities enable users to search by a combination of access points of a single kind, for example, two subject headings, as well as a combination of different access types, for example, subject and format of material. Thus, the user can retrieve materials on, say, FOOTBALL and TELEVISION as well as materials on football which are in a videotape format. In the first example, Boolean operators such as *and, or,* and *not* allow a patron to qualify a search involving terms which are equal in importance. In the second example, a search involving a primary term (e.g., a subject heading) can be limited by qualifiers such as format and date. While not useful as access points in their own right, the qualifiers can assist in defining the search according to characteristics, a factor which can be just as important to the user as the primary subject term.

The two generic capabilities described above have important implications for the retrieval of nonbook materials. It is now possible for users to query the catalog using access qualifiers particularly suited to nonbook characteristics, for example, by format of material, by type of equipment needed for use, and by running time, color, and similar specific attributes. It is now easier to expand the number of access points related to "authorship" responsibilities, in effect extending our definition of "author" to include the producer, director, performer, or other type of creator. In addition, persons or corporate bodies with publication or production responsibilities, such as producer, distributor, and production agency, can be included as main or qualifying access points.

Such kinds of sophisticated access help address some key questions which have traditionally been cited as problems in the cataloging of nonbook materials and, thus, as obstacles in their integration into a multimedia catalog. These questions involve the problem of diffuse authorship and of defining differing roles of authorship responsibility: How do we define who the author or authors are, or who is responsible for many types of nonverbal creations? How do we deal with the problem of diffuse authorship responsibility, where different authors have contributed in different ways to the creation of a work?[1] In part, some of these problems are diminished:

1. if the bibliographic record includes all of the "major" (if such can be defined) types of authorship responsibilities
2. if access is possible under any or all of these types of authors.

Identification by type of material is of crucial importance to many users seeking nonbook materials in the library's catalog. Another key and controversial issue in the cataloging of nonbook materials has involved the designation of format. How should the catalog inform the user of format or type of material? Material designators, color coding of cards, and separate catalogs for different formats are among the solutions which have been proposed at various times. It is now possible for online systems to allow a user to narrow a search by format. Thus, the user can restrict a search for *Hamlet* to sound recordings of the play or to videorecordings of a performance. In this way, the catalog can recognize two hitherto conflicting objectives: (1) informing the user of what the library has on a given subject or by a given author regardless of format, and (2) allowing the user to limit a search to a particular kind of format, or other characteristic, such as running time, size, color, etc.

### Access by Classification Notation

The opportunities that OPACs present for searching by classification notation can provide a new dimension for access to nonbook materials. Previously, classification systems were regarded primarily as location identifiers. Because of their physical differences from books, nonprint items were intershelved only in rare exceptions, eliminating the possibility for browsing by classification order.[2] With the capability for classification search in the catalog, nonbook materials can now be even more fully integrated into bibliographic systems. While many shortcomings of classification access have been pointed out,[3] classification still remains an access approach with enormous potential, allowing as it does the possibility for hierarchical searching as well as a search less susceptible to changes in subject terminology.

*Access by Keyword and by Truncated Form
of a Search Term*

Keyword access, which allows access to any term within a heading, and truncation, which allows access to part of a term, can be of particular value in searching for nonbook materials with a high incidence of generic titles, for example, *Map of Chicago.* Another commonly encountered problem with many nonbook materials, especially filmstrips and motion pictures, is titles beginning with phrases such as *Walt Disney presents . . .*, in which a statement of responsibility precedes the title.[4] Access under key words of the title can help alleviate such problems by providing access under any significant word or words of the title.

Keyword and title truncation can also be of assistance in instances where variant titles appear on differing parts of an item, a situation commonly the case with many nonbook items. Since many kinds of nonbook materials are best identified to the user by title rather than author, mechanisms which facilitate title access can be of special value in retrieval.

One prototype which incorporates many of the above-mentioned capabilities is FORMAT, a national computerized information system for Canadian nonbook materials. Using *AACR2*, the PRECIS subject indexing system, and MARC coding as standards for records processed by the UTLAS database, the FORMAT system offers Boolean search capabilities on 18 different fields of information, including title, series, language, type of material, color or black and white, date, abstract, running time, producer, director, distributor, production agency, and PRECIS subject index. The fields can be searched singly or in combination. The system thus enables a request such as "videocassettes on the subject of nuclear energy between 20 and 30 minutes in length, produced in the 1980s." Plans for future development include the addition of other searchable fields, such as all production credits, cast, and subject classification scheme. Also planned is an IBM-PC compatible version of the online catalog search software, and the distribution of portions of the database for loading into local microcomputer-based systems.[5]

While the FORMAT system represents a level of sophistication yet to be achieved in most OPACs, it indicates a potential for utilization of information already extant in most machine-readable records (if we substitute Library of Congress or Sears subject headings for PRECIS) and is an extension of features of access already common to many OPACs currently in use in libraries and other information centers.

If searching capabilities are to reach their fullest potential, further developments will be necessary not only on technological fronts, but also in the area of bibliographic standards. While present standards make it possible to search separate elements of bibliographic records and separate parts of a subject heading, it is not currently possible to retrieve parts of a classification notation. In the Dewey Decimal Classification, form subdivisions can be added by the classifier to indicate the type of material, but the present MARC format does not distinguish between parts of a Dewey number. Proposals have been made by Wajenberg and Cochrane to break down parts of Dewey numbers in the MARC format.[6]

Other types of changes will be needed to provide more up-to-date treatment for emerging technologies such as computer software. In a recent article, Joan Mitchell describes proposed revisions to the Dewey Decimal Classification and the Library of Congress subject headings as well as recent adoptions to *AACR2* and the Machine-Readable Data Files Format which will allow catalogers to provide potential access points more closely suited to developing computer formats.[7]

## Emerging Technologies

Current use of technology in the development of OPACs has enabled nonbook materials to become more fully integrated into multimedia databases. It has provided more sophisticated means of access to bibliographic records through the utilization of system features developed primarily for the retrieval and display of books and booklike materials. Future uses of technology, however, suggest retrieval and display modes which take advantage of unique characteristics of some nonverbal media.

Some future uses of technology are in pilot stages of development, and others are still in the planning stages. Nevertheless, the rapid development and application of recent technologies and the theoretical feasibility of implementation invite us to glimpse into the not-too-distant future, and to consider new directions for access and display of nonbook materials.

The unique contributions that such emerging technologies can make can be more fully appreciated if we consider modes of identification of some nonbook materials and the means by which some media communicate their message. In contrast to the verbal medium of book materials, many nonbook formats have as their "content" a visual or aural image which serves not only to express the artistic or intellectual content of a work, but also, in many cases, is remembered by the user more readily than a verbal label or title. If these visual or aural attributes are exploited in addition to traditional means of verbal access, such as author and title, new possibilities are presented for the effective identification, retrieval, and display of data for many nonbook materials. For example, in the case of known-item searching, many people can identify a picture more readily by its visual image than by its author or title. In music, the user may identify a work more easily if he or she can retrieve the work by its beginning melodic theme, or primary theme. In searching for maps, the coordinates can provide a much more precise and unequivocal access mode than the name of the geographic area.

In addition to providing access to items with which the user is already familiar, such methods can also help to serve the "choosing" function of the catalog for those who are browsing among like items. Seeing the graphic image of a visual item, or the notation for a theme, can assist the user in selecting from a collection.

### The Ultimate Subject Description

For static graphic items, such as pictures, posters, and slides, the viewing of the document or work itself represents the ultimate subject representation. A display of the document gives the viewer a description of the subject without the distortion resulting from translation and interpretation into verbal terms. Such complete subject description is possible with static graphic images, such as pictures and maps, because the item itself is discrete and noncontinuous, in comparison to media such as books, motion pictures, and sound recordings, which are designed to be viewed or heard in a continuum. With static graphic images, the message conveyed by the item is simultaneous and nonlinear, that is, capable of being grasped and comprehended at once.[8]

At present, some projects which employ the medium of videodisc, though largely in the experimental stage, hold promise of offering "complete subject description" for static graphic images.

The idea of graphic representation in a catalog is not new. Irvine outlines the history of graphic card catalogs and points out that a contact print catalog was developed at Harvard in the 1920s. Graphic card catalogs have been developed to provide access to certain visual media using various methods of photographic reproduction.[9] With the advent of optical disk/videodisc and laser disk storage and retrieval technology comes the capability of higher quality reproduction in an online, interactive mode.

The value of laser disks as an information storage and access medium lies in their ability to:

1. store images (both pictorial and textual) and sound
2. store large quantities of information in a relatively small amount of space, for example, 54,000 individual images on one side of a disk
3. allow random access to individual frames
4. allow instantaneous retrieval and display of images with viewer control via keyboard, hand-held commander, or touch-sensitive screens.

One experimental program utilizing videodisc technology is the Library of Congress' optical disk pilot program, designed to provide access to parts of the Library's collections. Since June 1984, patrons in the Prints and Photographs Reading Room have been able to browse, through a video monitor, a collection of almost 40,000 photographs, posters, architectural drawings, and other pictorial items. Images can be displayed automatically at a rate of several per second, or manually, with the user controlling the rate at which the images appear.[10]

Other disks in the experimental program will include other pictorial materials, such as picture publicity stills, color films and film segments, and television newscasts, to be stored on analog optical disks. The digital optical disk pilot program will store print images, including manuscripts, maps, and music as well as regular print materials.[11]

A similar project for storage and display of graphic images is in progress at the National Library of Medicine. Not surprisingly, librarians of visual arts collections have been in the forefront of experimentation with videodisc technology. In a recent article, Markey describes various earlier projects employing computerized information retrieval of images stored on videodisc in university and museum collections.[12] At the Avery Architectural and Fine Arts Library, Columbia University, a project is under way to catalog 45,000 architectural drawings on RLIN, store the images on disk, and provide topical access through the Art and Architecture Thesaurus subject headings. Users will be able to conduct a search at an RLIN PC terminal and retrieve both a cataloging record and a video image of the drawing described, or, alternatively, to browse through collections of images and then retrieve the corresponding bibliographic records.[13]

While videodisc technology offers considerable promise for display and access of graphic images, technological developments need to be accompanied by advances in the development of standardized formats for verbal description and access. The recently issued MARC format for visual materials, designed to accommodate two-dimensional materials in the films format, represents a significant advance which will make possible the creation and distribution of machine-readable records for art prints, pictures, posters, and similar materials.[14]

The Library of Congress' nonprint videodisc program was begun before the adoption of an approved MARC format for visual collections, but LC will prepare new records and test automated retrieval using what are called *captions*—records structured in a manner similar to the preliminary MARC format for visual materials. Captions will contain basic descriptive textual data, such as name of creator, title, date of creation, storage location of original image, and subject terms, and this information will be stored as a database in a microcomputer equipped with a software retrieval package. Two search modes will be thus be possible. Researchers can:

1. search the textual database by creator or subject access points, and retrieve corresponding image descriptions, to be displayed by the videodisc player
2. search by browsing through pictures on a videoscreen, and request textual descriptions for items of interest.[15]

The use of computer mapping technology for the retrieval and display of cartographic images provides another possibility for offering "complete subject description" of an item through graphic representation. In a prototype system developed for the Denver Public Library, data from census tapes and recent survey data are combined with maps of Colorado. At a color display terminal, users may browse the collection and choose maps according to geographic and other variables. Desired maps can then be displayed on the screen and copies printed out on request.[16]

While graphic images can be displayed, described, and browsed by means of the medium's own mode of communication, access other than browsing will in most cases continue to be provided in a verbal/textual mode. For maps and musical media, however, there is the possibility of providing access using descriptors or notation unique to the medium itself. In the case of maps, online retrieval systems can permit searches using geographical coordinates as access points. Such means of retrieval provide a precise and unequivocal identification of geographic entities, and are not subject to changes in boundary lines and place names. In addition, this mode of identification allows access to cartographic images which cannot be conveniently divided up into geographic boundaries.

The present MARC format for maps contains a field for the inclusion of coded mathematical data such as scale and coordinates. Possible uses for such a field are suggested by prototype systems which provide access under geographic coordinates of latitude and longitude. One example is a retrieval system used by the Earth Resources Observation System (EROS) Data Facility, under the administraton of the U.S. Geological Survey. The EROS data base contains over 1,000,000 items describing more than 6,000,000 aerial photographs and satellite images.[17]

In the case of musical compositions, access to a work through the notation for its musical incipit (opening theme) or by its main identifying theme likewise provides an alternate mode of access which describes the work in its own "language" and often with greater accuracy than by composer or title. Thematic indexes such as Barlow and Morgenstern's *Dictionary of Musical Themes* and Parson's *Directory of Tunes and Musical Themes* are examples of printed indexes which have used the incipit, represented by letters of the alphabet, as a means of retrieving citations to individual musical compositions.[18] Such tools are useful in cases where the composer or title of a work is not known, but a melody can be identified. Thus, by recalling the opening notes of a composition (or its major theme), a searcher could retrieve informaton about a musical composition or recording. Applications for computer-based thematic index retrieval systems have been suggested by Miller and Miller, who propose inclusion of retrieval themes in the MARC format.[19] Including musical themes as one of the descriptive elements of a musical composition could also serve to describe the work in its own terms, in ways that traditional verbal subject description cannot approach. Such an inclusion can assist in the precise identification of a work, since a theme can serve to distinguish a work from others.

In addition to proposing a MARC field for incipits using alphabetic characters, Miller and Miller look even further ahead, by suggesting ways in which existing computer languages could be used to convert musical notation to the sounds they represent using a sound synthesizer.

## Conclusions

A look at the development of online public access technologies and their impact on nonbook materials reveals an interesting interplay between characteristics of nonbook formats which set these materials apart from the predominant medium of books and those characteristics which are commonly shared by all media.

A recognition of attributes common to all media made possible the development of shared bibliographic standards such as AACR2 and MARC. Such standards are at once postulated upon a common theoretical framework for description of bibliographic data and a recognition of the need to describe unique attributes of nonbook materials. The common framework and shared standards made possible the inclusion of nonbook materials into broad-based machine-readable databases, and thus allowed them to become an integral part of OPACs.

While standards ensured the inclusion of unique attributes of media in bibliographic records, sophisticated retrieval capabilities made it possible for catalogs to utilize these attributes as access points. Thus, retrieval features have allowed access points to be derived from parts of the bibliographic record previously inaccessible through the catalog, and this has resulted in search capabilities which will enable the user to take into account unique qualities of nonbook materials, such as format and running time.

In the past, traditional manual modes of access had limited the effectiveness of retrieval of nonbook materials because of basic differences in authorship responsibility patterns, publication patterns, a high incidence of generic titles, and the unique character of their subject content. With the introduction of more sophisticated features of access, there is a greater likelihood that many of the difficulties will be resolved.

Indeed, the key contribution of online bibliographic access for nonbook materials has been the improvement and enhancement of system features for access. Description, or the record that the user retrieves in executing an access command, remains essentially unchanged in present systems. It is this area that is most likely to be affected by the emerging technology of optical disk storage and display. With the capability of displaying to the user a graphic image of items, such as art works, architectural drawings, maps, and music, the catalog display mechanism will be able to describe nonverbal items in their own language, to replace or augment an interpretation or translation of the item into a textual summary.

As of the present, such developments as LC's optical disk program are still in the experimental stage, and while greater development of shared standards for access and description of these full-text images needs to be accomplished, the potential is still evident.

Even farther into the future might be access systems which provide retrieval through identifiers unique to the medium, such as the kinds of access points made possible by an incipit, or opening theme, of a musical composition.

Regardless of the eventual development of online systems for access to nonbook materials, one thing is clear: there is enormous potential for creating access and display systems which go far beyond the traditional book-based author, title, and subject modes of access, and which transcend the traditional brief annotation or contents summary note which has served in the past to describe a nonbook work. With the help of such powerful tools for retrieval and description may come a greater visibility for nonbook media, and a larger role for them in the collections of libraries and other information centers.

### Notes

1. For discussions of these and related questions, see: Martha M. Yee, "Integration of Nonbook Materials in *AACR2*," *Cataloging & Classification Quarterly* 3(Summer, 1983):1–18; and Carolyn O. Frost, "Bibliographic Concepts and Their Application to Nonbook Materials" in *Cataloging Nonbook Materials: Problems in Theory and Practice* (Littleton, Colo.: Libraries Unlimited, 1983).

2. Foremost among the advocates of integrated shelving of media is Jean Riddle Weihs. See her book *Accessible Storage of Nonbook Materials* (Phoenix, Ariz.: Oryx Press, 1984).

3. For a discussion of limitations of online classification access, see: Janet Swan Hill, "Online Classification Number Access: Some Practical Considerations," *Journal of Academic Librarianship* 10(March, 1984):17–22. A useful overview of the advantages of online classification access is presented in Elaine Svenonius' article "Use of Classification in Online Retrieval," *Library Resources & Technical Services* 27(Jan./March, 1983):76–87.

4. The Library of Congress rule interpretation for this type of situation instructs the cataloger not to consider such statements of responsibility as part of the title proper: *Cataloging Service Bulletin* 13(Summer, 1981):15.

5. Donald Bidd, Louise de Chevigny, and Margo Letourneau, "Computerized Information System Operates for A-V Materials," *Canadian Library Journal* 41(December, 1984):323–330.

6. Arnold Wajenberg, "MARC Coding of DDC for Subject Retrieval," *Information Technology and Libraries* 2(Sept., 1983):246–251; Pauline Cochrane and Karen Markey, "Preparing for the Use of Classification in Online Cataloging Systems and in Online Catalogs," *Information Technology and Libraries* 4(June, 1985):91–111.

7. Joan S. Mitchell, "Subject Access to Microcomputer Software," *Library Resources & Technical Services* 29(Jan./March, 1985):66–72.

8. A similar view was expressed by William Nugent in Pauline Cochrane's article, "Modern Subject Access in the Online Age, Lesson Five," *American Libraries* 15(June, 1984):441, 443. Nugent points out that books and motion pictures have a linear continuity, whereas images in a picture collection constitute a "non-

linear set of discrete and discontinuous items, each deserving individual subject access." In his article "Words in Their Place," Rudolf Arnheim argues, "a literary image grows through accretion by amendment; a pictorial image presents itself whole, in simultaneity." *The Journal of Typographic Research* 4(Summer, 1970):199–212.

9.  Betty Jo Irvine, *Slide Libraries: A Guide for Academic Institutions, Museums, and Special Collections* (Littleton, Colo: Libraries Unlimited, 1979), 129—131.

10.  "The Library of Congress Optical Disk Pilot Program" (press release, Washington, D.C.: June 20, 1984).

11.  Ellen Z. Zahn, "The Library of Congress Optical Disk Pilot Program; A Report on the Print Project Activities," *Library of Congress Information Bulletin* (Oct. 31, 1983), 374–376.

12.  Karen Markey, "Visual Arts Resources and Computers," in *Annual Review of Information Science and Technology*, vol. 19, ed. Martha E. Williams (White Plains, N.Y.: Knowledge Industry Publications, 1984), 271–309.

13.  Telephone conversation with Janet Parks, Avery Library, Sept. 5, 1985. The *Art and Architecture Thesaurus* is described in Toni Petersen's article, "The AAT: A Model for the Restructuring of LCSH," *The Journal of Academic Librarianship* 9(Sept., 1983):207–210.

14.  *Cataloging Service Bulletin* no. 28(Spring, 1985):39–40.

15.  Carl Fleischhauer, "The Library of Congress Optical Disk Pilot Program, Research Access and Use: The Key Facet of the Nonprint Optical Disk Experiment," *Library of Congress Information Bulletin* (Sept. 12, 1983), 312–316.

16.  Donna Koepp, "Map Collections in Public Libraries: A Brighter Future," *Wilson Library Bulletin* 60(Oct., 1985):28–32.

17.  Robert F. Jack, "EROS Main Image File: A Picture Perfect Database for Landsat Imagery and Aerial Photography," *Database* 7(Feb., 1984):32–52.

18.  Harold Barlow and Sam Morgenstern, *A Dictionary of Musical Themes*, rev. ed. (London: Faber & Faber, 1983); and Denys Parsons, *Directory of Tunes and Musical Themes* (Cambridge, England: S. Brown, 1975).

19.  Karen Miller and Patricia A. Miller, "Syncopation Automation: An Online Thematic Index," *Information Technology and Libraries* 1(Sept., 1982):270–274.

■

# ■ Current and Future Needs of the Catalog: A User's Perspective

by Leigh S. Estabrook

*Catalogers are often admonished for not seeing things from the user's perspective. Though we may be no more at fault than any other group of specialists, as professionals we are keenly aware of the criticism.*

*Leigh S. Estabrook, herself not a cataloger, tells us several funny stories in her exploration of the future of nonbook cataloging. Catalogers are cast neither as villains nor heroes. Rather, catalogers are urged to forget their role as information professional and asked to cross the invisible line separating catalogers from the lay public. Each of Estabrook's tales illustrates important user needs in the process of trying to locate desired items by means of catalogs—the kind of information we are trying to provide.*

*As Estabrook helps us see things from a different perspective, the complicated concepts explored in other chapters in this book take on more human proportions and the ultimate purpose of our efforts assumes a new shape. Its form will influence our ideals for the foreseeable future, and our success depends on how well we determine clearly and precisely what is needed.*

Some time ago a friend of mine, the mother of three teenagers, told me the following story. One Saturday evening she and her husband found themselves in the enviable and most unusual situation of having all the kids away for the night. As they wandered about their home alone, the two decided that the way to spend the evening was to rent an "adult movie" to watch on their video cassette recorder. The problem was, they didn't quite know how to go about it. When they arrived at the video store, the only movies

Leigh S. Estabrook is Dean of the Graduate School of Library & Information Science, University of Illinois at Urbana-Champaign and author of "The Human Dimension of the Catalog: Concepts & Constraints" in the January/March 1983 issue of *LRTS*, pages 68–75.

they saw were ones such as *Conan the Barbarian*, several Clint Eastwood flicks, and *Jane Fonda's Workout*. The catalog of movies for the store listed nothing with an "X" rating next to it. The woman was convinced they didn't carry such movies, while the man was sure they did. Evidently, they wandered around the shop for quite some time, whispering to each other about whether two forty-year-olds could bring themselves to walk up to the counter and ask the clerk if he had something like *The Devil in Miss Jones*.

Finally, the woman went next door to a pay telephone and called the video store. The clerk told her they had adult movies and how to rent them. With information in hand, the man went back and followed the prescribed ritual of showing the clerk his rental membership card and requesting the "adult list." But that is not the end of the story. The adult list, it turned out, was not simply a list. It also had descriptions and reviews of films (not only written but also pictorial). It was difficult for the man to find information about the films because there were all those pictures of nude women interspersed with quotes from reviews. The one he chose was selected because *The National Review* called it the best porno movie made.

The story, however apocryphal, seems to describe well the issues that confront users of nonbook materials that should be considered in making such materials available. First, the story shows it is not always clear that what a user wants is available. Second, one often has difficulty knowing how to ask for what is wanted. Third, the type of information contained in a catalog of nonbook material is often distracting. Finally, the users for whom the catalog is developed may not be those who use it.

### Does It Exist?

Let me begin with the problem that users have in knowing whether what they want is available or, in fact, even exists. Rapid technological developments in all forms of nonbook material—from computer hardware and software to the use of chrome audio tape—often outpace even the experts in a field. Recently, I heard the director of a major computer center, an extremely knowledgeable man, deny the existence of a system that would combine words and graphics. Such a system was being used by several newspapers at that very moment. It was not in use, however, on the types of systems with which this academic computing czar was working. Users of any of these media will be aware of some things that are available, but may be completely blind to others.

Lack of knowledge of systems is an even greater problem for

casual users. Several years ago, for example, I bought an Osborne computer, principally for use as a word processor. It came with *Wordstar* word processing software and an inadequate manual about how to use that program. A year later, a colleague mentioned to me something called a "speller"—a software package that could check the spelling of text on the computer. Sometime after that it was brought to my attention that I could buy that software for use on the Osborne. Had it not been for these encounters with other users, it would probably never have occurred to me that spellers existed, nor that such a system could be used on my single-density, typing-case-sized machine. Without that knowledge, even the most sophisticated cataloging would be of little use. One must have reason to believe something exists and some vague mental image of what that thing might look like before beginning to look for it.

Catalogers who work with instructional nonbook materials are particularly challenged by this problem. Teachers may have a clear understanding of their learning objectives. They may know, for example, that they want to develop student understanding of organizational behavior. They may also know that having students read about this subject in a book may not be as effective as having them learn about it in some other way. Few of these teachers of management may know that *The Organization Game* exists and is effective in teaching organizational behavior to students at different levels.

### How Can I Retrieve It?

The second, and related, problem is that a user usually needs to know how to ask for something in order to retrieve it. To return to my "speller" example, if I had not originally heard of this type of program referred to as a "speller" or "dictionary" I might have begun with the idea that I wanted a program that would proofread my articles. I might even have thought that I was looking for a different word processing package. I didn't realize, initially, that I could first write using *Wordstar* and then run a different program to check the spelling.

Perhaps a better example of this problem is the story that Jeff Katzer, the interim dean at the School of Information Studies, Syracuse University, tells. When he was conducting a workshop for reference librarians in the California State Library System, the group ended up one day by telling stories about reference interviews that had gone awry. The story, as I recall it, went like this:

A woman came to the library asking if they had any material on a certain French painter. The reference librarian said they did and asked if the client was interested in some particular painting. To this, the woman said yes, and gave the name of the painting. The reference librarian then determined that the person wanted to see a copy of the painting. When that was found, the client looked at it and said thank you and began to leave. For some reason—and I don't remember how things went—the woman was intercepted and asked by another librarian whether her query had been satisfied. After much discussion, including questions regarding why the woman wanted to see the painting, the librarian discovered that the client was a painter who wanted to make a copy of the painting and wanted to know what size it should be. Every source and every copy of the painting that she had seen gave the dimensions in centimeters and she wanted to know its size in inches.

This is, of course, a classic reference problem made more acute by the variety of material forms now available in libraries. With nonbook materials, articulation of need may be particularly indirect because often a user seeks to satisfy some pedagogical purpose (e.g., to teach students about organizations). How that need should be satisfied may depend on the teacher's style, the type of students, and even the educational approach of the school. Even if I, as a user, get as far as asking for an experiential exercise to teach students about organizations, and in my subconscious I know that it can't be too "touchy/feely," how can I translate that request into a form addressed by the catalog?

## Distractions in the Catalog

The third point that the adult film story illustrates is that information in a catalog is often distracting for the user (remember the nude women?). Attempts to meet the needs of a diverse user population (and in fact to solve the problems just discussed), as well as to be precise, result in cataloging records that are incredibly detailed. For any one user much of that information may be irrelevant.

## Who Is Using the Catalog Anyway?

The fourth point of the adult film saga is that the users for whom the catalog is developed may not be the people who use it. I assume the video store catalog, which contained only nude young women (no nude young men), was based on a certain mental image of who would look at that catalog to select movies. The standardization of cataloging for nonbook materials reflects the cataloger's image of the various users and how those users might be expected to go about searching for the materials being cataloged.

To summarize briefly, for users of nonbook materials:

1. It is not always clear that what you want is available.
2. A user may have difficulty knowing how to ask for what is wanted.
3. The type of information contained in a catalog of nonbook material is often distracting.
4. The users for whom the catalog is developed may not be the people who ultimately use it.

### The Goals of Cataloging

The question we might consider is why these problems exist for users of nonbook materials in libraries. First, the goals of the cataloger are at odds with those of the user in at least one respect. The goals of the nonbook cataloger are the same as those of catalogers of any type of print materials—to describe the item as unique. This has been the goal of catalogers for centuries. What the cataloger seeks to do is to provide all descriptive elements necessary for someone else to ascertain that the information applies to one item and that item alone. This focus on describing the item as unique is most appropriate in cataloging rare books or differentiating one edition from another. For many users of nonbook materials, the problem is not whether an item is unique, but rather whether it is similar. For example, can this software be used on both an Apple and an Osborne? Can I play this new chrome tape on my old fashioned audio system? For many users it doesn't even help to say something is MS-DOS configured for Z-80 machines. What they need to know is: can they copy the disk, put it into their machine, and use it? The catalogers' approach to helping users ascertain whether works are similar—subject cataloging —cannot answer these types of questions.

A somewhat different problem arises for users of things such as kits. Users who order kits "new" on the market are sometimes dismayed to find that what they have bought is simply a newly packaged reissue of something bought several years ago.

As these examples indicate, the relationships between nonbook materials are more than "simple" author, title, or subject relationships—the traditional way for catalogers to link similar materials. Users need to know whether certain items are appropriate to answer a pedagogical goal. They want to know whether something that looks different is really the same.

## Are There Solutions?

The easiest solution, given current cataloging systems, seems to lie in increasing the number of record elements. But, as most catalogers admit, there are already enough elements with which to contend. MARC formatting requirements are not making it any easier. Faculty at the Nonbook Materials Institutes and those gathered at workshops have addressed the need for greater standardization. Research indicates, however, that nonbook cataloging is marked by a plethora of locally developed schemes, based on the needs of specific user groups. Such approaches address, in part, some of the problems I mentioned, but lead to others. A major problem is that users are not able to move between libraries or employ similar strategies in search of similar materials.

One alternative may be increased indexing. The Central New York United Way Oral History Project is one example of how this might work. Several years ago, they began to interview the people who had been instrumental in the formation and development of the United Way. Their purpose was to capture the flavor and character of the organization from material obtained from these interviews.[1]

Cataloging of the materials followed *AACR2* rules for sound recordings. The classification scheme used was ANSCR, the alphanumeric system for classification of sound recordings and the scheme used by the library which will receive the history once it is complete. The result is a series of entries in which the interviewee is the primary access point. Other information includes the name of the interviewer, recording format, date, length of time, etc.

The project is, however, more than a collection of interviews. It is, as I mentioned, intended to present a history of the events, places, and persons important to the development of the United Way. Project staff have developed an index and inventory of the recordings. This allows an historian wishing to obtain information about the first year of the United Way to identify the appropriate materials. It is not necessary for each researcher to listen to every tape.

I recognize that solutions such as these may seem out of the purview of cataloging. Moreover, some of my earlier points about making materials accessible may seem more appropriate to the reference staff. I would argue their pertinence to catalogers on several grounds. First, as you are well aware, the development and shape of library automation continues to break down that artificial barrier between technical and public services. Second, the types of problems encountered by the adult film seekers, by me, by the historians, or any other users are exactly those that information retrieval specialists are trying to address in system development. They are, in fact, the types of problems you are trying to address when you read this book.

## One Final Story

Let me conclude with one more story. In the past several years I have interviewed many librarians about the effects of technology on their jobs. The least satisfied of the group have been original catalogers of print materials working in academic libraries. The "fun" books (as one woman put it) are now being seen only by copy catalogers. The highly specialized technical reports and foreign-language materials that receive original cataloging are "boring" and, as another individual said, it is difficult to believe anyone will ever use the material.

Cataloging nonbook materials is the frontier. Many materials are "fun" and are desperately needed by users. However difficult the challenges, at least work with nonbook materials fights boredom.

### Notes

1. Pat Fletcher and Paul Shore, "Cataloging, Classification, and Related Aspects of an Oral History Project" (unpublished manuscript, Syracuse University, Dec. 1983).

# Part ■
## ■2

# Cataloging Individual Media

## Introduction

Half of each day during the Nonbook Materials Institutes was devoted to three-hour cataloging workshops. These sessions furnished practical hands-on experience in cataloging materials for various nonbook formats. Participants were afforded an opportunity to ask specific questions relating not only to the examples that were covered by each workshop leader, but also to problems they encountered in their day-to-day work back home.

Translating these unstructured sessions into chapters for inclusion here was a difficult task for the workshop leaders. Each session was unique, in that different questions arose and examples varied somewhat from one institute to another. In their workshops, each leader used the approach he or she found most useful and each worked in a different fashion, although they all covered similar territory. Capturing an entire workshop would have taken many more pages than are usually found in book chapters.

We believed that the information in the workshops was too important to omit. Despite all the difficulties, the workshop leaders were asked to develop chapter-length versions of a composite workshop drawn from all five of their presentations. They begin by discussing the general background of the medium or media group being covered and issues that are common to the cataloging of works in that medium. Then, explanations of specific examples (from the workbooks given to institute participants) highlight the main problems a cataloger will face when applying standard cataloging rules to items in that medium. Leaders were encouraged to use the approach that suited them best and, as a result, each chapter retains the flavor of the workshops on which it was based.

The organization of Part 2 follows the table of contents of the *Anglo-American Cataloguing Rules*, second edition. Our first chapter, by Richard Smiraglia, covers printed music and sound recordings, corresponding to chapter 5 and 6 of the cataloging code. Sheila Intner's chapter covering the cataloging of motion pictures and videorecordings relates to *AACR2*'s chapter 7. Lizbeth Bishoff combined in the treatments of two- and three-dimensional materials in her workshop, materials covered by *AACR2*'s chapters 8 and 10. Nancy Olson taught the cataloging of microcomputer software, subsumed in *AACR2* under chapter 9, with additional interpretations of those rules taken from the CC:DA guidelines for cataloging microcomputer software published in 1984.

The final workshop in this section, Sheila Intner's "MARC Tagging for Nonbook Materials," focuses on the application of conventions for encoding bibliographic information for computer entry and communication. It deals primarily with fields unique to those MARC formats developed for a selection of specific media groups, that is, Audiovisual Media (now called Visual Materials by the Library of Congress), Scores, Sound Recordings, and Machine-Readable Data Files.

In reading the chapters that follow, the fact that they represent standard practice at a particular point in time should be kept firmly in mind. Even as this book goes to press, proposals for changes to the cataloging rules, computer protocols, and other standard tools are being submitted, considered, approved, and implemented. Cataloging is a dynamic and evolutionary process, no less for nonbook materials than for books and printed serials. The underlying objective is, as always, to create ever more useful and effective systems of bibliographic control so that service to catalog users may be enhanced.

# ■ Cataloging Music and Sound Recordings Using *AACR2* Chapters 5 and 6

By Richard P. Smiraglia

Standards for the bibliographic control of music and sound recordings have followed roughly the same course as those for all other materials. Rules for music evolved from Oscar Sonneck's appendix on music in the 1906 edition of Cutter's *Rules for a Dictionary Catalog*.[1] The Music Library Association, formed in 1931, drafted rules in 1941[2]—later incorporated into the ALA/LC codes of the 1940s, and published separately under the aegis of both ALA and MLA in 1958.[3]

The 1958 MLA code saw the first appearance of rules for cataloging sound recordings, then referred to as *phonorecords*. Rules for sound recordings saw extensive revision as the medium developed. In 1964 a special publication containing the first revisions of these rules was issued by the Library of Congress. These rules eventually formed the content of the rules for phonorecords in *AACR*, chapter 14. One final revision took place before the publication of *AACR2*, a revision of chapter 14 published in 1976. This revision represented the first official appearance of the term *sound recording*.[4]

The International Association of Music Libraries *Code International de Catalogage de la Musique*, has appeared over several years, beginning in 1957 and reaching completion only in 1983.[5] This document had a major influence on the original ISBD (NBM) and ISBD (PM), which appeared in the mid-seventies. NBM will appear in a second edition within the next year or so. As *AACR* had largely incorporated the work of MLA and LC, *AACR2* expanded on these developments by incorporating many provisions of the ISBD documents.

At the time of *AACR2*'s publication, many issues in music cataloging remained unresolved. Since that time the process of reaching resolution of many of these issues has caused many revisions to *AACR2* in chapters 5 and 6. Additionally, there are over seventy-five separate rule interpretations issued in *Cataloging Service Bulletin* that apply to music materials and sound recordings.[6] Because many revisions are still before the Joint Steering Committee for the Revision of AACR, this chapter provides general guidance for cataloging music and sound recordings. Readers are cautioned to follow the *Cataloging Service Bulletin* for announcements concerning revised rules.

This chapter covers three areas: (1) descriptive cataloging of scores and sound recordings; (2) choice of entry for sound recordings; and (3) construction of uniform titles for musical works. Because form of entry is no different for music materials than for any other materials, it will not be specifically addressed in this chapter. Though this chapter is predominantly about music materials, some spoken word recordings appear among the examples at the end because chapter 6 must be used to catalog all sound recordings. Musical video recordings should be cataloged according to the provisions of chapter 7 of *AACR2* because they are essentially visual materials. However, the guidelines below for transcribing musical titles should be observed, and appropriate added entries for the musical works and performers should be made as set out below for sound recordings entered under title.

Many decisions that must be made in the course of cataloging music materials require specialized knowledge of music literature and bibliography. More detailed guidance for cataloging music materials, along with advice on how to obtain a basic familiarity with the literature, can be found in *Cataloging Music.*[7] Information concerning music cataloging also appears in the monthly *Music Cataloging Bulletin* in a column provided by the Music Section, Descriptive Cataloging Division at the Library of Congress.[8] "Music Cataloging Decisions," which are like rule interpretations but are issued by the Music Section rather than the Office for Descriptive Cataloging Policy, appear only in *Music Cataloging Bulletin.*

## Problems in Description

### Chief Source of Information

As with all nonbook materials the choice of the chief source of information is the first decision a cataloger must make. Printed music, because it follows in the tradition of the printed book, often appears with a title page. When a regular title page is present, it is used as the chief source. When one is not, the cataloger must choose whichever of the caption or cover provides the fullest information. The caption is the information which appears above the first measures on the first page of the music. In choosing a cover title the cataloger must not be misled by decorative title pages, also traditional in music printing. A cover must be made of substantially heavier material than the paper on which the music is printed, and in general a cover will not have music printed on its verso.

When a title page is present, but it consists of a list of works with the title information for the item in hand underlined or otherwise indicated, this is what is known as a "list" title page. Rule 5.0B1 instructs the cataloger to choose whichever of the list, the cover or the caption, furnishes the more complete information. Whichever source is chosen, if it is not a title page, must be indicated in a note.

For sound recordings, the labels on the recordings serve collectively as the chief source of information. However, when the recording is an anthology and the container provides a collective title that the labels themselves do not, rule 6.0B1 allows the cataloger to prefer the container as the chief source of information. It is important to remember that the name of a performer, if presented prominently, can be considered to be the collective title of a sound recording.

Catalogers of sound recordings may also wish to consider a hidden option at rule 6.1G. If a recording containing works by different persons or bodies has no collective title, the cataloger may choose to make a separate description for each *work* on the recording. If this option is chosen, the separate descriptions are linked by *with* notes. The Library of Congress has chosen to provide *unit* cataloging for all such recordings, but the option remains viable and most networks will allow bibliographic records prepared in either fashion to coexist in their databases.

*Area 1: Title, Statement of Responsibility, GMD*

For printed music and musical sound recordings, the next decision concerns the nature of the title proper. If the title consists of the name of a type of composition (such as *Sonata* or *Concerto*) then statements such as opus number, key, date of composition, and medium of performance are transcribed as part of the title proper. If the title is not the name of a type of composition (a title such as *Carmen*) or if it includes a modifier (such as *Little suite*), then such statements are transcribed as other title information. When it is not clear whether or not a term is the name of a type of composition, a source such as the *Harvard Dictionary of Music* can be consulted.[9] If the term is defined there, it is safe to assume that it is the name of a type of composition and should be treated accordingly. This is the type of title music catalogers refer to as "generic." For nonmusical sound recordings, the title area is transcribed as instructed in chapter 1 of AACR2.

Statements of responsibility are transcribed in the standard way, as instructed in chapter 1, for printed music. The cataloger should be on the lookout for statements in the chief source of information that indicate the present version is an arrangement (such as *Piano score*) even when no name is associated with the statement. Such statements are statements of responsibility and should be transcribed in area 1.

For sound recordings, the name of the composer of music, or the author of text, is routinely transcribed in the statement of responsibility. Performers' names are transcribed according to the guidelines at rule 6.1F1, which instruct the cataloger to include names of performers whose participation goes "beyond [mere] performance, execution, or interpretation of the work."[10] In other words, names of actors who have improvised their dialogue, or musicians whose performance has been largely improvisatory (as is the case with most kinds of "popular" music), should be transcribed in the statement of responsibility. Other performers' names are given in a note.

No general material designation (GMD) is used for printed music (an option decision from the Library of Congress), but the GMD *sound recording* is used for all recordings. When only one work is named in the title area (or when a collective title appears), the GMD appears at the end of the title proper. When two or more works by the same author or composer are recorded in the title area, the GMD follows all title information and appears immediately preceding the statement of responsibility. When works by more than one composer or author are recorded in the title area, the GMD falls at the end of area 1, following the last statement of responsibility. An example appears in the rules at 6.1G.

### Areas 2 and 3: Edition and Musical Presentation

Edition statements are not commonly found on musical publications. When they do appear they are given routinely in area 2 of the description. The cataloger should be careful not to confuse statements of responsibility (such as *piano edition*), which indicate a version or arrangement, or musical presentation statements (e.g., *Score and parts*, *Study score*, etc.), which indicate the physical format of the printed music, with edition statements (such as *Second edition*). Musical presentation statements are transcribed in area 3.

*Area 4: Details of Publication, Distribution, etc.*

According to a Library of Congress rule interpretation (1.4C7),[11] printed music is one of the categories of material for which the publisher's address is included in area 4, if it was issued by a U.S. publisher in the current three years and if no ISBN is present. Otherwise, area 4 is constructed in the same way it would be for books.

For sound recordings, the name given in area 4 must be the *label-name*, transcribed from the label of the recording. Often a single publisher (such as EMI) will own more than one label. The label-name (such as *His Master's Voice*) should be given in area 4 in such cases. When no place of publication is given on the item, the cataloger can often ascertain the location of a particular label from sources such as *Phonolog* or *Billboard . . . International Buyer's Guide.*[12]

Dates of publication can be troublesome for both music and recordings. For printed music, if the item has a plate number an approximate date can be ascertained by checking a source such as the plate number index (generated from MARC field 028) on either OCLC or RLIN.[13]

For sound recordings the cataloger should look for a copyright date which is preceded by the symbol ℗. The ℗ indicates the date of copyright of the *sound*. A © copyright date on a sound recording produced after 1971 indicates the date of copyright of the artwork or the notes on the container. If all else fails, these can be used to *estimate* a date of release for the recording, which should be given in brackets.

*Area 5: Physical Description*

For printed music the cataloger must determine the type of score in hand. Each of the terms in the list at 5.5B1 is defined in the glossary of *AACR2*. One should bear in mind that a *score* is "a notation showing all the parts of an ensemble . . . arranged one underneath the other on different staves. . . ."[14] If the music is only for one performer, it is not a score and is described as "p. of music." *Miniature scores* are scores that have been printed with small type, generally to be used as study scores, regardless of the height of the spine. If the type is too small to be conducted from, the item should be described as a *miniature score*. The term *vocal score* is used only to describe works for voices and instruments (usually orchestra) where the instrumental parts have been rewritten for a keyboard (usually piano). Music written originally for voice and piano is described as *score*.

Sound recordings are described as *1 sound disc, 1 sound cassette*, etc. The extent of the item is indicated by transcribing the duration in parentheses if it appears on the item. If no duration is given for the recording, do not attempt to estimate one. Other physical details include designation of the playback characteristics (analog or digital), the playing speed for analog discs (or cassettes when the speed is not the standard 1 ⅞ ips), and the number of sound channels (mono., stereo., quad., etc.) when given on the item.

If the cataloger has chosen the option of making separate descriptions for each work on a recording lacking a collective title, according to rule 6.1G, the extent of item is expressed according to the formula at rule 6.5B3. When the separately described parts are sequentially numbered or lettered, the expression *on side 4 of 3 sound discs* is used. When the separately described parts are not sequentially numbered, or are unnumbered, the form *on 1 side of 4 sound discs* is used. These expressions are followed by the durations of the corresponding separate parts, in parentheses, when the durations are stated on the item.

*Area 6: Series*

Most series are transcribed in routine fashion in area 6, as instructed in chapter 1 of *AACR2*. Catalogers of printed music should be careful not to confuse *publisher's numbers* that contain the name of the publisher with series statements. For example, *Kalmus orchestra library* is a series, but *Edition Peters* is a designation which occurs with a publisher's number.

Likewise, do not confuse a label-name on a sound recording with the name of a series. For instance, when the label says *Odyssey great performances*, then *Great performances* is a series; *Odyssey* is the label-name. In case of doubt, check the list of label-names in *Phonolog* or in the manufacturer's number index on OCLC or RLIN.

*Area 7: Notes*

Notes for scores include the following and are given in this order:

1. Form of composition and medium of performance, unless this is implied by the title or other title information

2. Language of sung or spoken text, unless it is implied by the language of the title proper
3. The source of the title proper
4. Variations in the title proper
5. Parallel titles and other title information
6. Statements of responsibility
7. Edition and history
8. Notation of the score, but only when it is an unusual type such as mensural, graphic, or klavaarskribbo
9. Publication, distribution
10. Duration of performance when it is given on the item. Always give the duration using digits, and separate the digits representing hours, minutes, and seconds by colons (e.g., 23:12).
11. Accompanying material
12. Series
13. Dissertation
14. Audience
15. Contents, but when all the items in a collection are of the same type of composition named in area 1, do not repeat that name in the contents note (see example at 5.7B18).
16. Plate and publisher's numbers. Plate numbers appear at the foot of each plate of music in a score, and should be transcribed exactly as they appear. If digits following a hyphen in a plate number correspond exactly to the number of plates (i.e., pages of printed music) in the item, these digits are not transcribed. Publisher's numbers have the same appearance as plate numbers (or in some cases they look like series) but appear only on the cover, title page, or first page of music. If both appear both are transcribed, the publisher's number given first.
17. Copy described and library's holdings.

Bibliographic records for sound recordings often require several notes. The same types of notes are made for recordings as for scores, but the order is slightly different. Give the following notes when applicable, in the following order:

1. Manufacturer's number. Give the label-name exactly as it appears in area 4 and the number which follows it on the label. This is given first according to a Library of Congress rule interpretation (6.7B19) because it is vital discographical information[15]

2. Artistic form and medium of performance
3. Language of sung or spoken text
4. Source of title proper
5. Variations in title, including differing versions of the title that appear on the container or in the notes
6. Parallel titles and other title information, including any that appear in different places on the item
7. Statements of responsibility, including the names of principal performers who were not named in area 1 unless their names are to be given in the contents note (see below)
8. Edition and history, including the place and date of recording if given in the accompanying text
9. Publication, distribution
10. Physical description, including the durations of the individual works unless these are included in the contents note (see below)
11. Accompanying material, including the presence of program notes if they are lengthy or unique. Only make a note if the program notes convey information which could not be located in standard reference sources.
12. Series
13. Dissertation
14. Audience
15. Other formats available
16. Summary, for nonmusical sound recordings
17. Contents, including where possible the durations of the individual works and the names of performers who perform in only one work on a recording. If the performer performs the entire recording, give the name in a statement of responsibility note (see above).
18. Copy described and library's holdings
19. With notes, giving the title and statement of responsibility of each separately described part of a sound recording with no collective title, when this option has been chosen according to rule 6.1G.

## Problems in Choice of Access

### Printed Music

The choice of access points for printed music follows the same principles that are applied to books. That is, the composer of music is considered to be the personal author and is therefore assigned main entry under the provisions of rules 21.1A and 21.4A. For musical works that include words (songs, operas, etc.), the composer is considered to be the principal personal author and again is assigned main entry status according to rules 21.1A and 21.19. Librettos, publications which reproduce only the words of a musical work (usually an opera), are entered according to the alternate rule at 21.28A, footnote 7 (by decision of the Library of Congress). This means that when reference is made to the musical setting, the libretto is entered under the heading for the musical work, with added entries for the librettist and any text on which the libretto may have been based. Special subrules for ballad operas, ballets, added accompaniments, and liturgical music appear at 21.19 and are self-explanatory.

Arrangements, musical works that have been rewritten for a different medium of performance, are entered under the heading for the original composition according to rule 21.18B. An added entry is made under the heading for the arranger. Adaptations, new compositions that are based on other music, are entered under the heading for the composer of the adaptation according to rule 21.18C. An added entry is made under the heading for the music on which the adaptation is based.

Care must be exercised that the term *arrangement* as used with music in popular idioms (jazz, rock, etc.) is not confused with the use of the term in Western art music. When the term is used with popular music, it should be understood to mean *composition* or *orchestration*.

Care should also be taken when entering anthologies of popular music (referred to as *pop-folios*). These publications are often written transcriptions of sound recordings. Usually, the chief source of information includes the title of the corresponding record album and the name of the featured performer. Though the recording may have been entered under the heading for the performer, the cataloger should check the statements of responsibility for each song to ascertain who composed the music in each case. Often, the songs are not composed by the performer named in the chief source, but rather are composed by a variety of people. As such, these collections receive main entry under title according to rule 21.7A. Added entries are made under the heading for the first-named composer, and under the heading for the performer (according to rule 21.29B).

*Sound Recordings*

Special rules, which balance the contributions of composers or authors and performers, are provided for the entry of sound recordings. Rule 21.1B2e provides for main entry under the heading for a corporate body when the responsibility of the group goes beyond simply performing a written work. This provision should be applied only in cases where the group has been chiefly responsible for the intellectual content of the recording. The Library of Congress rule interpretation for 21.1B2e cites the example of "an acting group that performs by means of improvisation. . . . The development of the drama proceeds entirely on the basis of improvised dialogue."[16]

For all other sound recordings, musical or nonmusical, rule 21.23 should be consulted. When the recording contains only one work, main entry is under the heading for that work, according to rule 21.23A. Likewise, when the recording contains more than one work by the same person, main entry is under the heading for that person, according to rule 21.23B.

Rules 21.23C–D apply to recordings which are collections of works by more than one person. For recordings that have collective titles, main entry is under the heading for the principal performer, according to rule 21.23C. A principal performer is a person or corporate body whose name is given prominence by the wording or layout of the chief source of information. If all the performers on a recording are given equal prominence, all are considered to be principal performers, and the rule of three applies. That is, when there are two or three principal performers, main entry is under the heading for the first-named with added entries under the others. When there are four or more principal performers, or no principal performers (i.e., when no performers are named in the chief source of information), main entry is under the collective title.

When a recording of more than one work by different persons or bodies has no collective title, rule 21.23D applies. If such a recording has been cataloged as a unit according to rule 6.1G, the choice of main entry is dependent on the nature of the recorded performance. If the works are of the type in which the performers have contributed more than simple performance of a written work, main entry is under the heading for the principal performer, the first of two or three principal performers, or the heading appropriate to the first work if there are four or more or no principal performers, according to rule 21.23D1. Added entries are made for additional principal performers and for up to twenty-five musical works if they require no more than fifteen analytical added entries and if the music is Western art music.[17]

For all other recordings, main entry is under the heading appropriate to the first work. Added entries are made according to the provisions outlined above.

Title added entries are always made for all distinctive titles on musical works. However, for nondistinctive titles, rule 21.30J4 prohibits title added entries when a conventionalized uniform title has been used.

## Music Uniform Titles

Uniform titles play an essential role in enabling the identifying and collocating functions of the catalog by both drawing together all variant manifestations of a work and distinguishing similarly titled but different works entered under the same personal name heading. Almost all musical works require uniform titles because of the great variety of titles proper under which manifestations of musical works appear.[18] Except for the rare cases in which the title proper of a given item is identical with the uniform title that it would be assigned (in which case no uniform title is used in the bibliographic record[19]), uniform titles must be formulated for all music bibliographic records. The process of formulating a uniform title for a musical work is fairly complex. Rules for formulating music uniform titles appear at 25.25–25.36 in *AACR2*. The discussion that follows outlines the steps that are applicable in all cases.[20]

*Choosing the Basis for the Uniform Title*
A uniform title for a musical work is based on "the composer's original title in the language in which it was formulated, [unless] a later title in the same language is better known," in which case it is preferred.[21] Except for recent compositions that can be ascertained to have appeared in only one manifestation, the original title and any later, better known versions in the same language must be determined from reference sources. For the purposes of formulating uniform titles, reference sources in the language used by the composer must be consulted.[22] For major composers, thematic catalogs may provide the fastest verification of the original title of a work. Thematic catalogs authorized by the Library of Congress for use with *AACR2* are listed in the *Music Cataloging Bulletin* and are cited in the Library of Congress name-authority file records for the composers.

*Manipulation of the Title*

Once the basis for the uniform title is chosen, the list at rule 25.26A is used to strip away excess terms such as medium of performance, key, opus number, etc. (This is the same process applied in title transcription according to rule 5.1B1.) For example, *Piano Sonata no. 1 in C major, opus 17* is rendered *Sonata*. This is referred to as the initial title element.

If the initial title element is distinctive, it is used as is. Initial articles, however, are deleted according to a Library of Congress rule interpretation.[23]

If the initial title element is not distinctive, that is, if it is the name of a type of composition, it is manipulated further to form a uniform title. Rules applied at this stage appear at 25.27B–25.31A6. If the nondistinctive initial title element is a term that is cognate in English, French, German, and Italian, the English form is preferred. If the composer has written more than one work of this type of composition, the English plural form is used. At this stage, the title of the aforementioned piano sonata is rendered *Sonatas*.

*Additions to Nondistinctive Initial Title Elements*

The next step is to add terms indicating the medium of performance, numbering, and key, as appropriate, to make the uniform title unique. Medium of performance is added according to the rules at 25.29, unless the medium of performance is implied by the initial title element (as is the case for *Symphony*, which implies orchestra, or *Chorale prelude*, which implies organ). Medium of performance is also excluded if no medium was designated by the composer, if the work is one of a set of works for differing media, or if the complexities of stating the medium make some other arrangement more useful. An example of the latter situation is the list of Mozart works titled *Divertimento*. There are many of these works, and alphabetical subarrangement by medium of performance would make the file difficult to access, so the medium of performance is not given and the thematic index number is used for subarrangement. In such cases, instructions to this effect appear in Library of Congress name-authority file records.

Additions for medium of performance are made using English-language terms whenever possible. Except for chamber music, no more than three terms may be used. This means that the terms for groups of instruments listed in 25.29E–F must frequently be consulted. The number of instruments is given parenthetically following the name of the instrument, unless the number is implied by other elements of the uniform title. Instruments are listed in the following order: voices, keyboard if more than one nonkeyboard instrument, and the order of other instruments in score order. Standard score order can be ascertained from the *Harvard Dictionary of Music*.[24]

Standard chamber music combinations are addressed by rule 25.29C. If the work is titled *Trio, Quartet,* or *Quintet* and is for the combination listed in parentheses, formulate the uniform title as indicated in the right-hand column of rule 25.29C. If the title of the work is not *Trio, Quartet,* or *Quintet,* use as the designation of medium the term indicated in the left-hand column at rule 25.29C. For all other works titled *Trio, Quartet,* or *Quintet* which are not for one of the standard chamber combinations listed at rule 25.29C, list all the instruments even if it means using more than three elements.

Other additions are made according to the rules at 25.31. These include as many as are applicable of the following: serial number, opus number or thematic index number (if a thematic index number is used the serial number is deleted), and key or tonal center. If these elements are not available or fail to create a unique uniform title, other elements may be added according to rule 25.31A6. At this stage, the uniform title for the aforementioned piano sonata has become: *Sonatas, piano, no. 1, op. 17, C major.*

### Additions to Resolve Distinctive Title Conflicts

If the title of the work is a distinctive title and it conflicts with the title of another work by the same composer, use rule 25.31B1 to add either a statement of medium of performance or a descriptive word or phrase. If this fails to resolve the conflict, add one of the elements specified at rule 25.31A, as described above.

### Uniform Titles for Excerpts

Unlike uniform titles for textual materials, uniform titles for musical excerpts are always constructed using the uniform title for the *whole* work, a full stop, and a designation for the part of the work. The designation of the part may be a number, a title, or both depending on the construction of the larger work. Detailed instructions are given in rule 25.32.

### Additions That Indicate the Manifestation

If the work being cataloged is not the composer's original, but rather an arrangement or a version of the original work, additions are made to indicate the manifestation in hand. These include the symbol *arr.* to indicate *arrangement*, the terms *vocal score, chorus score,* or *libretto* where applicable, a term indicating some other alteration of a musico-dramatic work, or the language of liturgical works or translations of other vocal works. These rules are found at 25.31B2–7.

### Collective Uniform Titles

Collective uniform titles are formulated according to the rules at 25.34–25.36. If the item contains all the works of a composer, the uniform title *Works* is used according to rule 25.34. If it contains three or more works of various types for various media, the uniform title *Selections* is used according to rule 25.35. If the collection consists of works of various types in one medium of performance, the medium of performance is used as the uniform title, according to rule 25.36A. If the works are all of one type of composition, the name of the type of composition is used as the uniform title, according to rule 25.36B. Finally, if the collection entered under 25.36A or 25.36B is incomplete, the term *Selections* is added, according to rule 25.36C, unless the selections form a consecutively numbered group, in which case the numerical designation is preferred.

## Examples

### Figure 1

Figure 1 is a miniature score of a concerto for orchestra. The medium of performance is considered part of the title proper because *Concerto* is the name of a type of composition. The musical presentation statement *Score* is transcribed in area 3. Though this score is the standard height of 31 cm., it is described as miniature score because the print has been reduced.

---

Figure 1

Sessions, Roger, 1896–
   [Concertos, orchestra]
   Concerto for orchestra / Roger Sessions. — Score. — Bryn Mawr : Merion Music : T. Presser Co., sole representative, c1983.
   1 miniature score (48 p.) ; 31 cm.
   Duration: ca. 15:00.
   Pl. no.: 446-41042.
   $35.00.

---

The uniform title is formulated by using the term *Concertos* because this composer has written more than one concerto. The medium of performance is added according to rule 25.29F. No further identifying elements are available. No title added entry is made because a conventionalized uniform title has been used (see rule 21.30J4).

Figure 2
The example in figure 2 is a vocal score of an opera. The title is distinctive, so the transcription of the title page is much like that for a book. The specific material designation is 1 *vocal score* because the original orchestral accompaniment has been arranged for piano.

Main entry is under the heading for the composer, with added entries under the headings for the librettists and for the work on which the libretto was based. Translators receive added entries according to rule 21.30K.

The uniform title is the original title of the work, which is distinctive. *Vocal score* is added to indicate the manifestation, and the languages are added because this score includes a translation.

---

Figure 2

Puccini, Giacomo, 1858–1924.
    [Bohème. Vocal score. English & Italian]
    La Bohème : based on "La vie de Bohème" by Henry Murger : an opera in four acts / libretto by Giuseppe Giacosa and Luigi Illica ; music by Giacomo Puccini ; with the original Italian text and the English version by Ruth and Thomas Martin. — New York : G. Schirmer, c1954.
    1 vocal score (vi, 292 p.) ; 27 cm.
    Publisher's no.: Ed. 2142.
    Pl. no.: 42660.
    I. Giacosa, Giuseppe, 1847–1906. II. Illica, Luigi, 1857–1919. III. Martin, Ruth Berenice Kelley, 1914–    . IV. Martin, Thomas Philipp, 1909–    . V. Murger, Henri, 1822–1861. Scènes de la vie de Bohème. VI. Title.

---

Figure 3
A set of score and parts are shown in figure 3. Bagatelle is the name of a type of composition, so the medium of performance is included in the title proper. The musical presentation statement is transcribed in area 3. Though this score is small, the print is standard, so it is not described as a miniature score. The desig-

nation of parts is added to area 5. The medium of performance is given as the first note. If a library's readers were accustomed to reading French, this might be considered redundant. The publisher's number (which appears only on the title page) is given before the plate numbers for both score and parts.

---

Figure 3

Dubois, Pierre Max, 1930–
    [Bagatelles, trumpets (3)]
    Cinq bagatelles pour trompettes / Pierre Max Dubois. — Partition [et] partiés. — Paris : A. Leduc, c1963.
    1 score (12 p.) ; 21 cm. + 3 parts ; 27 cm.
    For 3 trumpets.
    Duration: ca. 8:00.
    Publisher's no.: B.L. 891.
    Pl. no.: A.L.23.335—A.L.23.336.

---

*Figure 4*

The item in figure 4 is an example of a pop-folio. This anthology contains music from a motion picture. Main entry is under title according to rule 21.7B, with added entries under the headings for Nelson and Haggard and under the uniform title for the motion picture, according to rule 21.30G.

---

Figure 4

Pancho and Lefty / Merle Haggard ; Willie Nelson. — [U. S.] : H. Leonard Pub. Corp. and Columbia Pictures Publications, c1983.
    1 score (48 p.) : ports. (some col.) ; 31 cm.
    Songs, as sung by Haggard and Nelson in the motion picture of the same title; for voice and piano with chord symbols and guitar chord diagrams; words printed also as text.
    Contents: Pancho and Lefty / words and music by Townes Van Zandt — It's my lazy day / words and music by Smiley Burnette — No reason to quit / words and music by Dean Holloway — My Mary / words and music by Stuart Hamblen — My life's been a pleasure / words and music by Jesse Ashlock — Half a man / words and music by Willie Nelson — Reasons to quit / words and music by Merle Haggard — Still water runs the deepest / words and music by Jesse Ashlock — All the soft places to fall / words and music by Leona Williams — Opportunity to cry / words and music by Willie Nelson.
    Publisher's no.: PO462SMX.
    ISBN 0-89898-229-4 : $9.95.
    I. Van Zandt, Townes. II. Nelson, Willie, 1923–    . III. Haggard, Merle. IV. Pancho and Lefty (Motion picture).

*Figure 5*

In Figure 5, two sets of cataloging appear for the standard twelve-inch LP of Canon in D Major by Johann Pachelbel. There is no collective title, so figure 5a shows the unit cataloging as it would be constructed by the Library of Congress, and figure 5b shows cataloging for the separate parts, which is an option according to rule 6.1G.

In each case, the label-name *London Jubilee* is preferred to the name of the publisher, *Decca*, in area 4. The statements of responsibility for the performers are not included in area 1 but are given in a note, according to rules 6.1F1 and 6.7B6.

In figure 5a main entry is under the heading for the first work, according to rule 21.23D2, because there is no collective title. Added entries are made under the headings for the other performers and for the three musical works.

Note that in the first record in figure 5b Münchinger receives two added entries. The first is for Münchinger as arranger of the Canon. The second is for Münchinger as conductor of the performance. In a machine-readable record, these would be encoded differently and would therefore appear in different indexes in an online catalog. In a card catalog, the second entry would be superfluous.

---

Figure 5a

Pachelbel, Johann, 1653–1706.
    [Canon, violins (3), continuo, D major; arr.]
    Canon in D major / Pachelbel ; arr. Münchinger. The four seasons / Vivaldi. Adagio in G minor for strings and organ / Albinoni ; arr. Giazotto from original fragments and figured bass by Albinoni [sound recording]. — London : London Jubilee, [1979].
    1 sound disc (53 min.) : analog, 33 1/3 rpm, stereo. ; 12 in.
    London Jubilee: JL 41007.
    Title on container: Kanon / Pachelbel. The four seasons / Vivaldi. Adagio / Albinoni.
    Karl Münchinger, conductor; Stuttgart Chamber Orchestra; Konstanty Kulka, violin; Igor Kipnis, harpsichord.
    "All selections . . . previously released."
    I. Münchinger, Karl. II. Kulka, Konstanty. III. Kipnis, Igor. IV. Stuttgarter Kammerorchester. V. Vivaldi, Antonio, 1678–1741. Cimento dell'armonia e dell'inventione. N. 1–4. VI. Albinoni, Tomaso, 1671–1750. Trio sonatas, violins, continuo, G minor. Adagio; arr.

Figure 5b

Pachelbel, Johann, 1653–1706.
  [Canon, violins (3), continuo, D major; arr.]
  Canon in D major [sound recording] / Pachelbel ; arr. Münchinger. —
[London] : London Jubilee, [1979].
    on side 1 of 1 disc (4 min., 28 sec.) : analog, 33 1/3 rpm, stereo. ;
12 in.
    London Jubilee: JL 41007.
    Title on container: Kanon / Pachelbel.
    Karl Münchinger, conductor; Stuttgart Chamber Orchestra.
    "Previously released."
    I. Münchinger, Karl. II. Münchinger, Karl. III. Stuttgarter Kammeror-
chester.


Vivaldi, Antonio, 1678–1741.
  [Cimento dell'armonia e dell'inventione. N. 1–4]
  The four seasons [sound recording] / Vivaldi. — [London] : London
Jubilee, [1979].
    on sides 1 and 2 of 1 sound disc (40 min., 21 sec.) : analog, 33 1/3
rpm, stereo. ; 12 in.
    London Jubilee: JL 41007.
    Karl Münchinger, conductor; Stuttgart Chamber Orchestra; Konstanty
Kulka, violin; Igor Kipnis, harpsichord.
    "Previously released."
    I. Münchinger, Karl. II. Kulka, Konstanty. III. Kipnis, Igor. IV. Stutt-
garter Kammerorchester.


Albinoni, Tomaso, 1671–1750.
  [Trio sonatas, violins, continuo, G minor. Adagio; arr.]
  Adagio in G minor for strings and organ [sound recording] /
Albinoni ; arr. Giazotto from fragments and figured bass by Albinoni. —
[London] : London Jubilee, [1979].
    on side 2 of 1 disc (7 min., 14 sec.) : analog, 33 1/3 rpm, stereo. ;
12 in.
    London Jubilee: JL 41007.
    Karl Münchinger, conductor; Stuttgart Chamber Orchestra.
    "Previously released."
    I. Giazotto, Remo. II. Münchinger, Karl. III. Stuttgarter Kammeror-
chester.


*Figures 6 and 7*
  Two compact discs are used in figures 6 and 7. Figure 6 records
a single work with a distinctive title. Figure 7 is a recording with

a collective title, entered under the heading for the performing group, according to rule 21.23C. The term *indexed* is added to *Compact disc* in figure 6 because this is a special feature that is not available on all compact discs.

---

Figure 6

Holst, Gustav, 1874–1934.
  The planets [sound recording] : op. 32 / Gustav Holst. — West Germany : Deutsche Grammophon, p1981.
    1 sound disc (60 min.) : digital, stereo. ; 4 3/4 in.
    Deutsche Grammophon: 400 028-2.
    Orchestral suite.
    Parallel titles on container: Die Planeten = Les planètes = I pianeti.
    Berliner Philharmoniker; Herbert von Karajan, conductor; RIAS Kammerchor.
    Edition recorded: London : J. Curwen.
    Previously released as DGG 2532 019.
    Program notes in German, English, French and Italian in container.
    Compact disc (indexed).
    Contents: Mars (7:14) — Venus (8:34) — Mercury (4:11) — Jupiter (7:27) — Saturn (9:20) — Uranus (5:59) — Neptune (8:41).
    I. Karajan, Herbert von. II. Berliner Philharmoniker. III. Title. IV. Title: Die Planeten. V. Title: Les planètes. VI. Title: I pianeti.

---

Figure 7

Men at Work (Musical group).
  Business as usual [sound recording] / Men at Work. — N. Y., N. Y. : CBS Records, p1982.
    1 sound disc : digital, stereo. ; 4 3/4 in.
    CBS Records: CK 37978.
    Song texts in container.
    Contents: Who can it be now? ; I can see it in your eyes / C. Hay — Down under / C. Hay ; R. Strykert — Underground / C. Hay — Helpless automaton / G. Ham — People just love to play with words / R. Strykert — Be good Johnny / G. Ham ; C. Hay — Touching the untouchables / C. Hay ; R. Strykert — Catch a star / C. Hay — Down by the sea / C. Hay ; R. Strykert ; G. Ham ; J. Speiser.
    I. Title.

---

*Figure 8*
This popular music 45 rpm recording has no collective title, but is entered under the heading for the performer according to

rule 21.23D1. No analytical added entries are made for the songs because this is not Western art music.

---

Figure 8

Rogers, Kenny.
    I want to make you smile / Bill Medley ; [sung by] Kenny Rogers. Coward of the county / R. Bowling ; B. E. Wheeler ; [sung by] Kenny Rogers [sound recording]. — Los Angeles, Calif. : United Artists, p1979.
    1 sound disc (8 min.) ; analog, 45 rpm, stereo. ; 7 in.
    United Artists Records: UA-X1327-Y.
    From the United Artists album Kenny (UA LOO 979).
    Durations: 3:19; 4:18.
    I. Title. II. Title: Coward of the county.

---

*Figures 9 and 10*
Figures 9 and 10 are cataloging for spoken word recordings.

---

Figure 9

Mann, Thomas, 1875–1955.
    [Tod in Venedig. English]
    Death in Venice [sound recording] / Thomas Mann. — New York, N. Y. : Caedmon, p1982.
    2 sound discs (101 min.) : analog, 33 1/3 rpm, stereo. ; 12 in.
    Caedmon: TC 2090.
    Read by Jose Ferrer; directed by Ward Botsford.
    An abridgment of the translation from the German by T. T. Lowe-Porter, published: New York : A. A. Knopf, c1930.
    No tes by Thomas Lask on container.
    Summary: A story about a writer of world reknown and his slow spiral to a degrading sensuality and eventual death.
    I. Ferrer, Jose, 1912–     . II. Title.

---

Figure 10

Lambert, Thomas F.
    Tom on torts [sound recording] / Thomas F. Lambert. — [Washington, D. C.] : Association of Trial Lawyers of America, p1980.
    8 sound cassettes.
    Lectures.
    Intended audience: Lawyers.
    Contents: 1–2. Products liability overview — 3. Punitive damages. Damages — 4. Legal innovation and imagination — 5. Psychic injuries — 6–7. A tort law update — 8. Whither the civil jury?
    I. Association of Trial Lawyers of American. Education Fund. II. Title.

Figure 9 is a novel on two discs. Figure 10 is a series of lectures on eight cassettes. Note the different kinds of notes that are made for nonmusical recordings, particularly the *Summary* notes. Notice that figure 10 has only the extent of item in area 5. This is because all the other details of physical description are standard for the item.

## Notes

1. Oscar G. Sonneck, "Music," in *Rules for a Dictionary Catalog*, 4th ed. (Washington, D.C.: Govt. Printing Office, 1906), 138–140.

2. Music Library Association, *Code for Cataloging Music*, preliminary ed. (typescript, 1941).

3. Joint Committee of the Music Library Association and the Division of Cataloging and Classification, American Library Association, *Code for Cataloging Music and Phonorecords* (Chicago: American Library Association, 1958). Chapter I, "Entry and Heading," had appeared as rule number 12 of: American Library Association, *Cataloging Rules for Author and Title Entries*, 2nd ed. (Chicago: ALA, 1949); and, Chapter II, "Description," had appeared in Descriptive Cataloging Division, Library of Congress, *Rules for Descriptive Cataloging in the Library of Congress* (Washington, D.C.: LC, 1949), 75–96. Both chapters were revised for this 1958 publication.

4. See *Rules for Descriptive Cataloging in the Library of Congress: Phonorecords*, 2nd preliminary ed. (Washington, D.C.: Descriptive Cataloging Division, Processing Department, Library of Congress, 1964); "Chapter 14: Phonorecords," in *Anglo-American Cataloging Rules, North American Text* (Chicago: American Library Association, 1967); and *Anglo-American Cataloging Rules, North American Text: Chapter 14 Revised: Sound Recordings* (Chicago: American Library Association, 1976).

5. International Cataloging Code Commission, International Association of Music Libraries, *Code International de la Catalogage de la Musique* (Frankfurt: IAML, 1957–1983).

6. *Cataloging Service Bulletin* (Washington, D.C.: Cataloging Distribution Service, 1978–  ), quarterly.

7. See Richard P. Smiraglia, *Cataloging Music*, 2nd ed. (Lake Crystal, Minn.: Soldier Creek Press, 1987).

8. *Music Cataloging Bulletin* (Canton, Mass.: Music Library Association, 1969–  ), monthly.

9. Willi Apel, *Harvard Dictionary of Music*, 2nd ed., rev. and enl. (Cambridge, Mass.: Belknap Press of Harvard University Press, 1969).

10. *Anglo-American Cataloguing Rules*, 2nd ed., ed. Michael Gorman and Paul W. Winkler (Chicago: American Library Association, 1978), 149.

11. *Cataloging Service Bulletin*, 13 (Summer 1981):3.

12. See *Phonolog Reports* (Los Angeles: Phonolog Publishing Division, 1948–  ), loose-leaf; and *Billboard . . . International Buyer's Guide* (New York: Billboard Publications, 1962–  ), biannual.

13. See also Commission for Bibliographical Research, International Association of Music Libraries, *Guide for Dating Early Published Music: A Manual of*

*Bibliographical Practices*, comp. D. W. Krummel (Hackensack, N.J.: Joseph Boonin; Kassel: Bärenreiter Verlag, 1974).

14. Apel, *Harvard Dictionary*, 759.

15. *Cataloging Service Bulletin* 14 (Fall 1981):17.

16. *Cataloging Service Bulletin* 14 (Fall 1981):21.

17. See *Cataloging Service Bulletin* 28 (Spring 1985):14.

18. See Richard P. Smiraglia, "Toward Justifying the Use of Music Uniform Titles," (typescript, presented to the *Music Library Association Pre-Conference on Authority Control*, Louisville, Ky., 1985).

19. *Music Cataloging Bulletin* 13 (Jan. 1981):1–5.

20. For a more detailed discussion see Smiraglia, *Cataloging Music*.

21. *Anglo-American Cataloguing Rules*, 474.

22. In many cases *The New Grove Dictionary of Music and Musicians*, ed. Stanley Sadie, 20 v. (London: Macmillan; New York: Grove's Dictionaries, 1980) will do, but see also "Chapter 6: A Music Cataloger's Reference Collection," in Smiraglia, *Cataloging Music*.

23. *Cataloging Service Bulletin* 11 (Winter 1981):45–46.

24. Apel, *Harvard Dictionary*, 759.

# ■ Cataloging Motion Pictures and Videorecordings Using *AACR2* Chapter 7

by Sheila S. Intner

*AACR2* grouped chapters for the nonbook formats differently than did its predecessor, *AACR*, published in 1967. In *AACR*, Part III, motion pictures were part of a group that included slides, filmstrips, and other materials based on film and film products.[1] Videorecordings (called, simply, *videos* here) were still quite new to libraries during the late 1960s, and rules for cataloging them were not yet included in the code. However, by the early 1970s when code revision was under way, library collections of videos were beginning to flourish. By 1975, cataloging rules for them had already been devised and published, for example, in Weihs' *Nonbook Materials: The Organization of Integrated Collections* (1970, 1973)[2] and the AECT's *Standards for Cataloging Nonprint Materials* (1971, 1972).[3] Videos began to be included by the Library of Congress in its *LC Catalogs: Films and Other Materials for Projection* in the July-September 1976 issue.

The characteristic chosen to distinguish this format group in *AACR2* was not the reproduction of visual images or the material on which the visual information was recorded, that is, film. It was, rather, whether or not the images appeared to move when the item was played (or projected, or viewed, if you prefer). Thus, *motion pictures* were removed from their still film cousins and brought together with video, which also recorded visual images in motion, to form a separate chapter in *AACR2*—chapter 7.

The Library of Congress has been cataloging films since mid-century. Its rules for description of films, first published in 1952,[4] served as a foundation for the film rules in *AACR* and, later *AACR2*. However, no concerted efforts were made to achieve consistency with the rules for other cataloged materials, particularly books, until the 1970s, when librarians found that the lack of consistency in the book and nonbook chapters of *AACR* prevented them from integrating the entries into a unified multimedia catalog. (Jean Weihs comments on this situation in the first chapter, "A Taste of Nonbook History.") Sufficient consistency to integrate entries of books, films, and videos, if that was what a library desired, was achieved in the second edition. In part, it was the result of applying a uniform structure, that is, the ISBD structure, to all materials covered by the code; in part, it was the result of declaring at the outset that consistency was an objective worth achieving.

The ISBD structure provides the skeleton upon which all descriptive cataloging is built. The number (eight) and order of elements (title–edition–material specific details–details of publication–physical description–series–notes–standard numbers) is the same for films and videos as it is for every other kind of material. All the rules of chapter 1 apply to films and videos as well. Access points are chosen, for the most part, in exactly the same way (although there are some special rules which accommodate situations found primarily in the recordings of performances, sound or visual, and do not apply to other kinds of materials). But to create a bibliographic description for a film or video, beyond obeying the general structure of ISBD and rules of chapter 1, one must apply the rules of chapter 7 which furnish specific guidance in translating both for these particular media.

## Special Problems of Cataloging Film and Video

### Chief Source of Information

One problem of cataloging nonbook materials in general, and films and videos in particular, results from trying to fit their data sources into the title page mold. Most films and videos have multiple sources of bibliographic information. They have opening frames (also called title frames) which bear some resemblance to the title pages of books, usually containing the title and major credits for the work about to be seen. However, they also have closing frames with additional credits—extremely extensive in some instances—listing technical contributors (i.e., camera people, costumers, casting directors, etc.), performers, and, sometimes, persons or bodies responsible for the production and/or distribution of the work.

Opening and closing frames are not eye-readable. Catalogers need access to playback equipment to view them and, thus, to transcribe data from them (transcription from the item itself always being preferred for bibliographic information). The item in hand may also have eye-readable information on a container which cannot be separated from the rest of it (called an *integral container*). The cassette parts of videocassettes are examples of integral containers. Codemakers recognized such containers and the labels permanently affixed to them as equal to title and end frames, including them, too, in a complex set of data sources serving as chief source for chapter 7 materials.

If none of these preferred chief sources are available to catalogers, then substitutes can be selected. The code lists the following alternate chief sources, in order of preference: accompanying textual matter, containers not an integral part of the item, and other sources.[5] If an alternate data source is selected to substitute for inaccessible title frames, end frames, and integral containers and labels, it becomes the chief source and the information transcribed from it does not have to be bracketed. (Cataloging from alternate chief sources is a matter of necessity at LC, where much film and video cataloging is done from data sheets provided by producers/distributors. The results are likely to be far less accurate than if preferred chief sources were used, as they normally are for book cataloging.)

### Title, GMD, and Statement of Responsibility

Catalogers often find that the multiple data sources (i.e., opening and end credits, integral containers and labels) each contain different information for the same element of description. A common discrepancy is different titles proper on opening/closing frames and/or on several labels all permanently affixed to an integral container. One video currently being marketed to libraries has two different titles. *Abbott and Costello Live* is the title on two labels permanently affixed to the cassette. What does not show is a different title proper alternative displayed in the opening frames when the video is played: *The Colgate-Palmolive Comedy Hour.* Nowhere on the video itself is the label title displayed. Which title should be selected as title proper and which, if any, might be treated as a series title is a matter of choice.

This phenomenon, that is, that the person trying to catalog an item (whether originally or with existing copy) must make critical decisions, is what makes cataloging films and videos appear difficult.

Another problem frequently encountered with chapter 7 materials is long statements of responsibility linked to titles proper, for example, *J. Arthur Rank presents Laurence Olivier in Shakespeare's Hamlet.* Should this title proper begin at the beginning with *J.*, as it would if it were a book title (grammatically linked

Figure 1

*Data from the chief source of information:*

Columbia Pictures presents

Sean Connery

in a Robert M. Weitman Production

*The Anderson Tapes*

also starring

| Dyan | Martin | Alan |
|------|--------|------|
| Cannon | Balsam | King |

*Bibliographic Description:*

The Anderson tapes [videorecording] / produced by
Robert M. Weitman ; directed by Sidney Lumet ;
screenplay by Frank R. Pierson. — [Burbank,
Calif.] : Columbia Pictures Home Entertainment,
c1971.

1 videocassette (98 min.) : sd., col. ; 1/2 in.

Title from label.

Based on the novel by Lawrence Sanders.

Cast: Sean Connery, Dyan Cannon, Martin Balsam,
Alan King.

Credits: Music by Quincy Jones.

VHS format.

Summary: An ex-convict plots the robbery of an
entire apartment building while the authorities
monitor his movements with electronic devices.

I. Weitman, Robert M. II. Lumet, Sidney. III.
Pierson, Frank R. IV. Sanders, Lawrence. The An-
derson tapes. V. Connery, Sean. VI. Cannon, Dyan.
VII. Balsam, Martin. VIII. King, Alan.

sentences are transcribed as is), or after the last preposition, *Shakespeare's Hamlet,* or with the briefest possibility, *Hamlet?* LC established a rule interpretation (LCRI) other U.S. catalogers follow,
treating films and videos differently than books in this respect:
"When credits for performer, author, director, producer, presenter,
etc., precede or follow the title in the chief source, in general do
not consider them as part of the title proper, even though the
language used integrates the credits with the title."[6] The title
proper for the fictitious example above would be *Shakespeare's
Hamlet.* A real example of this common title proper problem occurs in figure 1.

The general material designations for chapter 7 items are *motion picture* and *videorecording*.[7] They should be bracketed following the title proper and are always given in the singular form.

Motion pictures and videos are almost always the product of many people and/or bodies who furnish different contributions to the whole. Deciding who should be named in the statement of responsibility (area 1) is not always easy. *AACR2* tells catalogers to record the names of persons or bodies participating in the production who are credited in the chief source and who are considered important to the cataloging agency.[8] Another LCRI gives guidance in applying this rule.[9] It directs catalogers to name persons or bodies with overall responsibility for the work in this area (e.g., producers, directors, writers, etc.) and those who are responsible only for one aspect of the work (e.g., performers, composers of music, costumers, etc.) in the notes (area 7). Only the principal persons or bodies with overall responsibility should be named in the catalog entry, not assistants, associates, or others named in subordinate positions.

Catalogers retain responsibility for determining exactly who are the producers (not always an easy task when several persons or bodies have titles that include the word *producer* or *production, producing,* etc.), director(s), and others appropriate for inclusion in area 1. The best way to do this is to become familiar with motion picture and video production, learning who does what in the industries and relying on reference sources as necessary to supply additional assistance.[10] There is no substitute for knowledge of the field.

### Material Specific Details

A proposal to use this area (area 3) for archival filmed materials to record an item's country of origin was accepted by cataloging authorities, but it is not applicable to nonarchival filmed materials.

### Publication, Distribution, etc.

In this area, as in the statement of responsibility, there is often confusion about which person(s) and body(ies) should be named. Motion pictures and videos are not published in the same sense of the word as are books. Unlike some other kinds of nonbook formats (e.g., sound recordings), doing the job of production does not necessarily include getting the finished products to the market. Producers and production companies for motion pictures and videos create the works, making intellectual and artistic contributions that make them comparable to authors and, therefore, worthy of listing in area 1. They work for other persons or bodies who control the release and distribution of the completed works. Releasing and distribution, for motion pictures and videos, is analogous to publication for books. Therefore, it is the releasing and/or distributing agent or agents that should be named in this area, whether persons, bodies, or both.

Another decision may be required to identify the appropriate corporate body or bodies for inclusion here. For one thing, in recent years, multinational conglomerates have purchased some well-known motion picture/video companies, adding the names of the parent companies to their subsidiaries'; for another, agreements between production companies and releasing and distributing agents may result in several of these names appearing on the item. A useful rule of thumb for catalogers is to transcribe the name or names of those bodies from whom additional copies of the item would be purchased were they desired. A library would not go to Gulf & Western (the parent company) to buy or lease a Columbia Pictures (the subsidiary) release. Catalogers need to think in like manner to work their way through any choice among several names, using knowledge of the motion picture and video industries or reference tools that provide trade information to identify the relationships among them.

Choosing the appropriate date from among many possibilities is a similar exercise. Completion of the production of a motion picture or video does not always signal its release (or distribution), which may not occur for months or even years. The date of release is preferred over other possibilities in this area. An LCRI offers guidance about recording copyright dates when a time lag of two years or more exists between the release and copyright dates. It states: "Give a date of original production differing from the dates of publication/distribution or copyright, etc., in the note area. . . . Apply the provision if the difference is greater than two years."[11]

*Physical Description*

Problems in the physical description area for motion picture and video materials relate mainly to newer subformats, especially videodiscs. Two specific problems predominate. First, catalogers need to decide when the brand name of associated hardware should be recorded in this area of description and when it should be put in the note area. Second, appropriate measurements for these materials, which were not anticipated in *AACR2's* original design, need to be determined and transcribed.

The test that determines if information about the hardware

brand should be included, in parentheses after the specific material designation, is whether there is only one system on which the item can be played. If there is, then the brand name is added to the physical description. If not, catalogers may decide to describe associated hardware in a note if this information is deemed important to users of the catalog records. Unfortunately, what sometimes happens when a new subformat is marketed is that there is only one playback system for a period of time until other manufacturers are able to respond to market demands by producing similar pieces of equipment. Catalogers following the recommendation may reach a point, such as happened with Umatic videocassettes, at which the one-to-one relationship between a type of material and playback system no longer holds. At this point the brand name should no longer be made part of the physical description.

The second problem, that of appropriate measures for new subformats, has been addressed by codemakers in the ongoing revision process. The most important of the provisions addresses the physical description of videodiscs, which do not play at uniform speeds. Catalogers are now directed to omit the information if it is not meaningful and if it is standard for the item.

### Notes

Notes for chapter 7 materials follow the same patterns, for the most part, as those in other chapters. If the title proper is not transcribed from the preferred chief source, then a note should be given to tell its source (7.7B3). When multiple, variant titles have been encountered in area 1, a note giving those not chosen as title proper should be made, especially if they are desired as access points (7.7B4). Cast and credits are recorded in the statement of responsibility note (7.7B6). Cast and credits notes should always be made for principal performers and production staff if the information is likely to be used by library clients or when the cataloging is being contributed to a bibliographic utility. (Fullness of records affects the value of the bibliographic utility's database to all participants.)

Another note often used in cataloging chapter 7 materials records edition and history (7.7B7). Many motion pictures and videos bear relationships with other works, for example, they may be based on novels or plays, or they may be recordings of live performances. Similarly, notes are necessary to furnish useful background when multiple releases, sometimes with changes of title, dubbed sound tracks, or other major differences are involved.

Figure 2

First summary of *Casablanca*:

13 520    A woman must choose between escaping with her husband from Nazi-controlled Vichy France territory, Morroco, or staying behind with her ex-lover.

Second summary of *Casablanca*:

13 520    A story of the struggle between diverse individuals who have sought refuge in Casablanca after fleeing Nazi-occupied Europe during World War II.

Physical description notes (7.7B10) should be made to record the type of equipment necessary to play or project the item, unless it is obvious from information already given in area 5. Since there is no way to distinguish between Beta and VHS videocassettes in area 5, that information should be recorded in this note. Additional information about the physical medium (i.e., film or tape, sound, etc.) is appropriately given here, too.

Summaries of the contents of motion pictures and videos are extremely important and should be given carefully and thoughtfully. One reason is that these materials can rarely be browsed and selections are usually made on the basis of catalog entries. Another reason is that similar titles (or even identical titles) for very different works are not infrequently encountered among motion pictures and videos. Well-written summaries, however brief they may be, may be the only way catalog users can distinguish among them. Sometimes, a single item may be given very different summaries by different catalogers. Figure 2 shows notes from two OCLC records for the classic motion picture *Casablanca*, each offering its own version of the plot.

Audience level notes ought to be made only if that information is given on the item itself and after consideration about the possible value of the item to people other than the recommended audience. Works intended for children are sometimes just as useful for adults (and vice versa), but a statement saying *For grades 4 through 6* on something could effectively deter adults from using it.

*Access Points*

Most motion pictures and videos are the result of many people or companies making different contributions—intellectual, artistic, and technical—to complete the production. Not only are these items the result of mixed responsibility, but often more than three separate contributors are involved. As a result, title main entry is frequently the choice made for these materials. That said, catalogers need to be aware that common occurrence of title main entries is not a universal law without exception. The same rules apply to the choice of main and added entries for these items as for all other materials. In addition, rule 21.1B2e permits corporate body main entry for motion pictures and videorecordings (as well as sound recordings) done by performing groups where the contribution of the group clearly constitutes the predominant responsibility for the work. In an item where the performing group were also the producers, directors, and writers as well as the performers, 21.1B2e would be invoked to assign the main entry to the group. (The Beatles' motion picture *The Yellow Submarine* is an example of this kind of interpretation.)

Added entries for those with overall responsibility for a motion picture or video is recommended, as well as for the principals in the cast and alternative titles, provided these entry points are important to users of the catalog entries.

These problems, while sometimes difficult to resolve, seem less formidable as one gains familiarity with the media and begins to recognize common practices in motion picture and video graphics, representation of performing and technical credits, and industry organization.

### Notes

1. "Chapter 12: Motion Pictures and Filmstrips," in *Anglo-American Cataloging Rules, North American Text* (Chicago: American Library Association, 1967), 282–293.

2. A preliminary edition of *Nonbook Materials* was published first in 1970, and, after a trial period during which it was applied by librarians in the North American community, it was revised and the first edition was brought out in 1973. Both editions were published by the Canadian Library Association.

3. The title of the first edition, published in 1968 by the Department of Audio-Visual Instruction of the National Education Association (DAVI/NEA), was *Standards for Cataloging, Coding and Scheduling Education Media*. DAVI was later superseded by the Association for Educational Communications and Technology, which published the 2nd and 3rd editions of *Standards*, with the title *Standards for Cataloging Nonprint Materials* in 1970, 1971, and later, a 4th edition in 1976 which remains the current edition.

4. *Rules for Descriptive Cataloging in the Library of Congress: Motion Pictures and Filmstrips*, preliminary ed. (Washington, D.C.: Library of Congress, Descriptive Cataloging Division, 1952).

5. *Anglo-American Cataloguing Rules*, 2nd ed., ed. Michael Gorman and Paul W. Winkler (Chicago: American Library Association, 1978), 166.

6. *Cataloging Service Bulletin* 13 (Summer 1981): 15.

7. *Anglo-American Cataloguing Rules*, 20.

8. *Anglo-American Cataloguing Rules*, 169.

9. *Cataloging Service Bulletin* 11 (Winter 1981): 15.

10. Some useful references are: *Halliwell's Film Guide*, 4th ed., rev. & updated (New York: Scribner, 1985); *The International Motion Picture Almanac* (New York: Quigley, 1929–    ), annual; *The International Television Almanac* (New York: Quigley, 1956–    ); *The Video Source Book*, 2nd ed. (Syosset, N.Y.: National Video Clearinghouse, 1979).

11. *Cataloging Service Bulletin* 15 (Winter 1982): 6.

# ■
# ■ Cataloging Two- and Three-dimensional Materials Using *AACR2* Chapters 8 and 10

by Lizbeth Bishoff

The rules for the descriptive cataloging of graphics and three-dimensional objects are covered in chapters 8 and 10 of the *Anglo-American Cataloguing Rules*. These materials, including puppets, puzzles, filmstrips, transparencies, etc., are typically left uncataloged, and often reside on a shelf in an office or get stored in a cabinet. Knowledge of the existence of the items is limited, with word of mouth being the primary method of providing access. Why aren't librarians cataloging two- and three-dimensional materials? Are they intimidated by the many different parts? Are they confused by multiple title pages or a nonexistent title-page equivalent? Is there too much or too little bibliographic information available? Should Dewey or Library of Congress classification numbers be provided? Are accession numbers better? Media codes? How about subject headings? And what about processing these materials? Where does the possession stamp go on a transparency or a puzzle part? Should each part of a game be labelled? Clearly, many questions arise that catalogers do not face when working with books. This should not dissuade us from cataloging these materials, entering them into the bibliographic databases, and circulating them to users just as books are cataloged, entered, and circulated.

*AACR2* has attempted to deal with the idiosyncracies of the various media, including two- and three-dimensional materials, while providing a basic set of rules for the bibliographic description of all materials a library would collect. Is it important to use this standard set of rules for cataloging these materials? It would appear advisable, as one of the major criticisms of *AACR* was the lack of rules for cataloging many nonbook formats and the resulting proliferation of nonstandard manuals and codes. As libraries move toward acquisition of a variety of media, cataloging nonbook materials and books with the same set of rules seems most logical. *AACR2* provides for consistent description of all materials so that catalog users are presented with information that is basically the same regardless of the type of material. A second reason for using national cataloging standards is the ability to use cataloging from other libraries, realizing economies and achieving staff efficiencies through shared cataloging systems.

As libraries move toward automating various systems, standardization is important. More and more libraries are participating directly or indirectly in OCLC, RLIN, or WLN for cataloging, and joining cooperative circulation systems or acquisition programs. Consistency in bibliographic data will result in improved access for clients and reduced cost to libraries for cataloging.

Let's look first at the cataloging of some of the media. This discussion is organized the way one would catalog, medium by medium, item by item. We will look at the special problems encountered with each of seventeen different media, focusing in each case on those elements of description that can be problematic.

Remember, with *AACR2* catalogers use chapter 1 and the chapter related to the particular medium. In fact, if someone only cataloged models, it would not be unreasonable for that person to break apart *AACR2*, keeping only chapters 1 and 10, 11 to 13, and 21 to 26. Chapters 2 through 9, being unused, could be discarded.

One important caveat should be kept in mind: Rules may not be "borrowed" freely from chapters that deal with types of media different from the item in hand. For example, although there are rules for locally produced sound recordings (called *nonprocessed* recordings) in chapter 6, they cannot be applied to locally produced graphics even though there are no rules in chapter 8 for such materials. Only the rules in chapter 1 and the specific chapter for graphics may be used.

## Problems in Cataloging Graphic Materials

### Art Original (Chapter 8)

When describing an art original, the cataloger needs to recognize that, in general, each item is unique. However, lithographs are considered art originals even though there are multiple copies.

The chief source of information for an art original is the item itself. The example in figure 1 is a framed color lithograph with water color highlights. A certificate of authenticity prepared by the art gallery distributing the lithograph appears on the back of the frame. This certificate carries title information. However, as

---

Figure 1
**Art original**

Hutchet.
  [Sunday sail] [art original] / Hutchet. — [197–?].
  1 art print : lithograph, col. ; 17 x 12 cm.
  Title on label affixed to the verso of the framed work.
1st of 25 prints, signed by the artist in pencil.
  Size when framed: 36 x 25 cm.
  I. Title.

---

this frame and backing are not permanently affixed to the work itself, this information is bracketed.

As the title information was not on the item itself or on a permanently affixed label, it is placed in brackets. The signature of the artist on the front, in pencil, is transcribed as it appears into the statement of responsibility.

*AACR2's* glossary provides definitions of the various general material designations. The only appropriate designation for this item would be *art original,* although the definition of *art print* in *AACR2's* glossary includes the term *lithograph.*

Rule 8.4A2 specifically states that for art originals, only the date is given. Information regarding distributor can be provided in this area if it is considered important; however, if the item is distributed by a local gallery, it might be more appropriate to put that information in the note area.

As for the physical description, the appropriate specific material designation is selected from the list in 8.5B1. In this case, it would be *art print.* Give as other physical details the process that is used for the print, that is, *lithograph,* and if it is in color or black and white. For dimensions, rule 8.5D4 instructs the cataloger to give the size of the art original, excluding the frame or mount.

Notes are given for the source of the title, as it was supplied by the cataloger, the edition and history of the item—specifically, the number of this lithograph in the series (EA I/XXV, which appears on the certificate)—and lastly, the size of the work when framed.

The main entry for the item is the heading for the artist. Further research was done on the artist, but no additional information was found in reference sources that might indicate the need for other, related added entries. An added entry is made for the title.

Figure 2
**Chart**

> Moncure, Jane Belk.
>     The life cycle of a frog [chart] : a
> sequence chart / by Jane Moncure ; illus-
> trations by Harry Moeller. — Elgin, Ill. :
> Child's World, c1971.
>     6 charts, 6 cards : col. ; in container,
> 32 x 48 cm. + 1 booklet.
>     Intended audience: For ages 8 and up.
>     A 6-panel sequential chart with re-
> source material on the backs of the panels.
> 6 duplicate cards for children to use in
> practicing sequencing.
>     I. Moeller, Harry, II. Title.

*Chart (Chapter 8)*

A chart is defined as "an opaque sheet that exhibits data in graphic or tabular form."[1] Frequently, charts will include text as well as graphic or tabular information.

*The Life Cycle of a Frog* (figure 2) has multiple parts—several large charts, several cards, and a booklet. According to 8.0B1, if an item has two or more separate physical parts and the items have a collective title, then the container serves as the chief source of information. The title and statement of responsibility as well as the details of publication, distribution, etc., are transcribed from this chief source of information.

*Chart* is one of the choices found in the list of general material designations for graphic materials.

In regard to physical description, rule 1.10C2 provides three ways to describe the physical format of multipart items. In this case each item is listed in paragraph format. The dimensions of the item are to be measured in centimeters. If there is a container, provide the measurement of the container before the accompanying material, with additional text describing the type of container, for example, *in box, in bag,* etc. Record the presence of accompanying material by naming the item and optionally providing the physical description information.

Age level and summary notes are generally helpful for audiovisual materials as these items cannot always be browsed as easily as printed materials.

The main entry for this item is the heading for the individual responsible for the intellectual content. This information is pro-

Figure 3
**Filmstrip (as dominant medium)**

    Friskey, Margaret.
       The little engine that could [filmstrip] /
    adapted by Margaret Friskey ; illustrated by
    Katherine Evans ; narrated by Donald Gallagher.
    — Chicago : Society for Visual Education, 1966.
       1 filmstrip (42 fr.) : col. ; 35 mm. +
    sound cassette (7 min.) + 1 teacher's guide. —
    (Children's fairy tales ; A 111-5)
       Side 2 of cassette: Rackety rabbit and the
    runaway Easter eggs.
       Based on the author's 1939 novel.
       I. Evans, Katherine. II. Gallagher, Donald.
    III. Series. IV. Title. V. Title: Rackety
    rabbit and the runaway Easter eggs.

vided on the item itself. Optionally, make an added entry under the name of the illustrator. Make an added entry for the title.

*Filmstrip (Chapter 8)*

Filmstrips are frequently combined with sound recordings in one of several formats—disc, cassette tape, etc. Whenever the cataloger is presented with a multipart item, the question of predominant medium arises. A rule of thumb for determining predominance is to ascertain whether the item can stand on its own. If the intellectual content was intended by its creator to be communicated by one part of a multipart item, then that part can be considered the dominant medium. If two different media are required to communicate the content, then the item is considered to be a kit.

A filmstrip is the dominant medium when the text of the filmstrip is printed on the frames, thus communicating the content even in the absence of the sound recording. The general material designation will be *filmstrip*. On the other hand, if there is no text on the frame and the explanation of the content of the filmstrip is provided by a sound recording, the intellectual content of the item cannot be conveyed by the filmstrip alone. In such a case, the item is considered a kit.

For a filmstrip, the chief source of information is the item itself, including labels that are permanently affixed to it, and a container that is an integral part of the item. In figure 3, the title, statement of responsibility, details of publication, distribution, etc., and the series statement are transcribed from various parts of the item. Occasionally, statements of responsibility are found at the end of the filmstrip or on another part of the item, such as the container or accompanying material. Be careful not to assign responsibility for the intellectual content of the item to the manufacturer, publisher, or distributor, unless the organization is truly responsible for the content.

Depending on the number of parts and the determination of a dominant medium, the general material designation is either *kit* or *filmstrip* (in this case *filmstrip*).

As to physical description, when the filmstrip is the predominant medium, describe the item in terms of the number of filmstrips followed by the number of frames. In the case of the example in figure 3, the sound recording and booklet are considered accompanying material because the filmstrip alone can convey the intellectual content. Provide information about the extent of these items according to the needs of the cataloging agency.

Notes for filmstrips frequently include summary notes, details on accompanying material, and contents. In our example, a note is made that a different title is recorded on side 2 of the cassette. The cataloger has the option of tracing that title, too.

The main entry for the item is the heading for the name of the adapter, whose name is provided by the chief source of information. If the author of the original work had differed, a name-title added entry for the original would be provided. In determining the main entry, the cataloger should be careful when circumstances seem to indicate the publisher or manufacturer should be assigned intellectual responsibility. If that is under consideration, rule 21.1B1 for main entry under a corporate body should be consulted.

An additional problem that catalogers may encounter in determining main entry responsibility is that of considering information provided in accompanying materials. Frequently, the credit appearing there is only for the accompanying material, not for other parts of the item. This information should be given in a note.

Added entries are provided for the illustrator, narrator, series title, and title proper.

*Flashcards (Chapter 8)*

In the example in figure 4, the container serves as the unifying element, bringing together the several parts and therefore is used as the chief source of information. Information used for the bib-

Figure 4
**Flashcards**

> Fenderson, Julia K.
>     The reading box [flashcard] : 150 reading games &
> activities / Julia K. Fenderson. — Rev. ed. — Carson,
> Calif. : Educational Insights, 1974.
>     154 cards : b&w ; 10 x 15 cm. in box.
>     Summary: "This Reading Box is intended as a source of
> a variety of supplementary aids, ideas and techniques for
> your reading programs."
>     Contents: Reading readiness — Listening skill builders
> — Vocabulary builders — Phonics — Choral verse — Read-
> ing through writing — Comprehension skills — Dramatic
> play — Dictionary and reference skills — Speed reading
> — Book reports — Continuum of reading skills.
>     Educational Insights: 9112.
>     I. Title.

liographic description is displayed in a variety of places on the
container. The title, statement of responsibility, and details of
publication are transcribed from the container. The edition statement is located on the end panel of the container.

*Flashcard* is one of the general material designations for
graphic materials.

Detail the number of cards and provide the dimensions of the
items and their container for the physical description.

Notes for this item include a summary note, which is a formal
note taken from the item itself; a contents note; and a note giving
the publisher's number, found on the item.

Personal responsibility is assigned to the creator of the flashcards, the heading for whom becomes the main entry. An added
entry is made for the title.

*Kit (Chapters 1 and 8)*
A kit is an item containing two or more categories of materials,
none of which is identified as the predominant medium. The
example in figure 5, *Recycling*, consists of items in three media—
a filmstrip, a sound cassette, and a pamphlet. Based on the facts
that the filmstrip does not have text on the individual frames and
the cassette is necessary to communicate the intellectual content
of the item, this item does not have a dominant medium. In cataloging the item, consult chapters 1 (1.0H and 1.10) and 8.

The various parts of the item are considered the chief source
of information rather than the container, since this container does

Figure 5
**Kit (using chapters 1 and 8)**

> Recycling [kit] : an ecology study / presented by
> the Aluminum Association. — New York : the
> Association, [1973?].
> 1 filmstrip (78 fr.) : col. ; 35 mm. in container,
> 31 x 32 x 6 cm. + 1 cassette (ca. 30 min.) + 1 tea-
> cher's guide + 1 booklet (45 p.).
> Booklet lists recycling centers.
> Cassette with audible and inaudible advance signals.
> I. Aluminum Association (United States).

not provide a collective title different from that provided on the items themselves. In this case, the title is found on the filmstrip, cassette, and pamphlet.

The general material designation for this item is *kit.*

In this case, the statement of responsibility is found on the last frame of the filmstrip.

As the publisher was previously named in the statement of responsibility, the name can be abbreviated.

Rule 1.10C2 provides three options for describing items in multiple parts. Separate physical descriptions for each part are provided for in the second option.

A note is provided for accompanying materials that are not included in the physical description. A second note indicates the requirement for playback equipment capable of handling an in-audible advance signal.

Main entry for this item is under title because it emanates from a corporate body, but it does not fall into one of the categories of material for which it is permissible to assign a corporate body main entry in rule 21.1B2. An added entry is made for the corporate body, and the qualifier *United States* is added to distinguish two bodies with the same name.

*Picture (Chapter 8)*

A picture is defined in *AACR2* as a two-dimensional visual representation accessible to the naked eye. Our example in figure 6, *19th century skills and crafts,* is a collection of 24 pictures stored in a portfolio-like container.

The portfolio and an explanatory sheet are the chief source of information for this item; they provide a collective title as well as the details of publication.

---

Figure 6
**Picture**

19th cent. skills and crafts [picture]. — Madison,
Wisc. : State Historical Society of Wisconsin,
c1976.
24 pictures : b&w ; 28 x 21 cm. in folder.
Pictures from the Iconographic Collections, State
Historical Society of Wisconsin.
I. Wisconsin. State Historical Society.

---

---

Figure 7
**Poster**

[Go for it!] [picture] : use your library. —
[Chicago : American Library Association,
1983.]
1 wall poster : col. ; 56 cm. in diameter.
Poster for the 1983 National Library Week promotion.
I. American Library Association. Public
Information Office. II. Title: Use your library.

---

*Picture* is selected from the list of general material designations.

A note describes the source of the pictures.

Access points for this item include main entry under title, with an added entry for the historical society.

*Poster (Chapter 8)*

A poster meets the *AACR2* description of a picture, that is, a two-dimensional visual representation accessible to the naked eye and generally on an opaque backing.

The item itself is the chief source of information. Additional information can be taken from the accompanying materials and other sources. In figure 7, a catalog is considered the other source.

*Picture* is one of the general material designations available for graphic materials.

Publication, distribution, etc., information is taken from the 1983 ALA National Library Week promotion catalog. As this source of information is not one of the prescribed sources for this area of description, the information is bracketed.

As for physical description, the specific material designation

Figure 8
**Slides**

> Bandelier National Monument [slide] : New Mexico. —
> New York : GAF, [19——].
> 5 slides : col. — (Pana-vue travel slides ; S319Q).
> Contents: Frijoles Canyon — Upper Falls — Pueblo
> of Tyuonyi ruins — Prehistoric cliff dwellings —
> Talus House.
> I. Series.

for this item is *wall poster*. The measurement is the diameter, given in centimeters.

A note describes the purpose of the poster.

Access points for this item include main entry under its title, another added entry under subtitle and an added entry for the American Library Association.

*Slide (Chapter 8)*

The slide set in figure 8 is composed of five slides distributed by GAF in a plastic carrier. The question it presents is: Since this is a multipart set, does the carrier serve as a unifying element providing a collective title when the items themselves do not? Each slide has a title and the statement *Bandelier Nat'l Monument*. The carrier, however, gives a more complete title, with the word *National* spelled out and a subtitle added.

As the carrier provides more complete detail, it is selected as the chief source of information.

One of the terms on the list of general material designations is *slide*.

Publication, distribution, etc., information is transcribed from the chief source of information, with a supplied date.

The extent of the item details the number of slides. An indication of color should be given. As slides are standard in dimension, the dimension need not be given. The rule for physical description instructs the cataloger to give the dimensions only if they are other than the standard size, i.e., 2 inches by 2 inches.

Provide a contents note, listing the specific title for each slide.

Access points include main entry under the title and an added entry for the series title.

*Viewmaster Slide (Chapter 8)*

Figure 9 illustrates cataloging for a Viewmaster slide. Viewmaster slides are special slides that are on a reel rather than a strip

Figure 9
**Slide (Viewmaster)**

> Walt Disney Productions presents Dumbo [slide]. —
> New York : Viewmaster/GAF, c1978.
> 3 stereograph reels (Viewmaster) (21 double
> fr.) : col. + 1 booklet.
> Title on container: Dumbo.
> View-Master: J-60.
> I. Walt Disney Productions. II. Title: Dumbo.

and are double framed. When viewed, these slides give the impression of three dimensions.

The chief source of information is the item itself. Generally, there is bibliographic information on the carrier or the label on the reel. Each set of slides comes in a paper jacket which can include bibliographic information, too. Prefer the information found on the item itself to that found on the jacket. Therefore, transcribe the title that is on the reel. An added entry is made for the title on the jacket.

*Slide* is the general material designation.

Publication, distribution, etc., information is transcribed from the chief source of information.

For physical description, the specific material designation *stereograph reels* is selected, with the extent of the item followed by information on the number of frames and the fact that they are double frames. Other details include the term *stereograph*. Dimensions are not given for this item, according to rule 8.5D3. Accompanying material is a small booklet.

The variant title on the container is given in a note. The manufacturer's number is also given in a note.

There are three access points. The item is entered under title, with an added entry for the container title. An added entry is also provided for the manufacturer.

*Transparency (Chapter 8)*

The set of transparencies in figure 10 presents the situation of a multipart item lacking a collective title on the item itself. The container and accompanying material do provide a collective title, even though the container does not serve as a unifying element.

The chief source of information is the item itself; however, information from the container and accompanying material are preferred in this case since they provide a collective title.

Figure 10
**Transparency**

> Park, Jeanne.
>      [Zoning the home for better family living]
> [transparency]. — St. Paul, Minn. : 3M, c1968.
>      20 transparencies (3 attached overlays) :
> col. ; 21 x 27 cm. + 1 contents sheet in con-
> tainer 34 x 28 x 4 cm. — (Home economics ; no.
> 32).
>      Title from container.
>      Transparencies are mounted.
>      3M: 3532.
>      I. Title. II. Series.

Select and transcribe the collective title from the container, enclosing it in square brackets. The statement of responsibility appears only on the contents sheet and nowhere else, so it is not transcribed.

The general material designation is *transparency*.

Publication, distribution, etc., information is provided on the mount of each slide as well as on the container.

For physical description, the rule that applies to the extent of item for transparencies includes directions for indicating the number of overlays. When describing the dimensions of transparencies, do not include the mount. This information is provided in a note.

Make a note indicating that the title is taken from the container. Notes giving the size of the transparency when mounted may be given if desired. A note is made for the manufacturer's number.

Access points include main entry under the heading for the creator, Jeanne Park. Added entries are made for the title and series.

## Problems in Cataloging Three-dimensional Artefacts and Realia

*Game (Chapter 10)*
A game is defined as a set of materials designed to be played according to a prescribed set of rules. How literally we interpret the "prescribed set of rules" may be a critical question. For example, a child's game where the task is to put a round block into a round hole may be considered a game by this definition, since

---

Figure 11
**Game**

> PacMan [game] : Tomy pocket game. — Japan :
> Tomy, [198–?].
> 1 pocket game : plastic ; 12 x 8 x 1 cm.
> Intended audience: For ages 3 and up.
> Tomy: 7015.
>     I. Tomy (Company).

---

there is only one way in which the block can be put into the hole, that is, it is prescribed. In other cases, a set of rules is provided with the game, clearly prescribing its play.

The item itself is the chief source of information, with accompanying textual materials and a container issued by the manufacturer. Information found on the item itself is preferred to other information.

*Game* is one of the general material designation options listed for three-dimensional materials.

In regards to the publication, distribution, etc., information, three-dimensional materials frequently have both manufacturers and distributors listed. In the case of *PacMan* in figure 11, we know the country in which the item was manufactured and the name of the manufacturer because it is impressed on the plastic container, but must supply an approximate date since none is given.

For the physical description, the specific material designation is to be as concise as possible, so in this case *pocket game* is used. The material of which the game is made is also given. The size of the item is given in centimeters.

Notes on the audience level and the manufacturer's number are provided.

Access points include title main entry, as the responsibility for its intellectual content is unknown, and an added entry for the manufacturer.

Another example of the application of the rules for games in chapter 10 is *Pigmania*, a game with multiple parts. In this case (figure 12), the box serves as a unifying element, providing more complete information than the various pieces.

The container is the chief source of information, as it provides more information than the parts.

*Game* is the general material designation.

For the physical description, a specific material designation is

Figure 12
**Game**

> Pigmania [game] : an original game of chance using
> pigs as dice. — Chicago : David Moffat Enter-
> prises, c1977.
>> 1 game (2 pigs, 1 cup, 1 pen, 1 pad of paper)
> in container, 13 x 24 x 8 cm. + 1 set of rules.
>> For 2 or more players, ages 6 to adult.
>> I. David Moffat Enterprises.

Figure 13
**Kit**

> Can I breathe the air? [kit]. — Cambridge, Mass. (1033
> Massachusetts Ave., Cambridge, MA 02138) : Urban
> Systems, c1970.
>> 1 vial calcium hydroxide, 1 carbon monoxide detector,
> 1 carbon monoxide chart, filter paper, filter holder, 1
> rubber bulb atomizer, 1 eye dropper, 1 booklet in con-
> tainer, 35 x 25 x 20 cm. — (Urban systems ecology kit ;
> 7)
>> Contains material for testing carbon dioxide, carbon
> monoxide, and sulfur dioxide.
>> I. Urban Systems.

selected and the number and names of the pieces are added to it,
in parentheses.

Notes giving the audience level and the recommended number
of players are provided.

Access points are title main entry, since the person responsible
for the intellectual content is unknown, and again an added entry
for the manufacturer.

*Kit (Chapters 1 and 10)*

When cataloging a kit, the cataloger needs to refer to rule 1.10
and the rules applicable to the media forms comprising the particular kit. For the example in figure 13, a chemical testing kit, the
rules of chapter 10 are applied in addition to 1.10.

The chief source of information is the container, as it serves
as the unifying element for a multipart item.

Choosing a specific general material designation is not possible, because there is more than one material type and none pre-
dominates. Consequently, the term *kit* is selected from the list.

---

Figure 14
**Model**

> Empire State Building [model] : New York City. —
> Hong Kong : Enco [National Corp.], [19—].
> 1 model : plastic, bronze ; 23 cm. high in box
> 23 x 8 x 6 cm.
>    Box contains facts about the Empire State Build-
> ing.
>      Enco 5-2192.

---

For the physical description, select one of the options provided
in 1.10C2, that is, provide the extent of each part ending with the
words *in container*.

A summary note explains the purpose of the kit.

As before, access points are main entry under the title, with
an optional added entry under the name of the producer.

*Model (Chapter 10)*

A model is a three-dimensional representation of a real thing,
either of the exact size or to scale. In figure 14, the model of the
Empire State Building is a scaled version of the real building.

The object itself, accompanying material, and the container
serve as the (multiple) chief source of information for this item.
Prefer information found on the item itself. Therefore, the title is
transcribed from the object. The subtitle is found on the container.

The term *model* is the general material designation.

Publication, distribution, etc., information is found on the container. The item's date of manufacture is unknown, except that it
is in the twentieth century. The name of the manufacturer—
Enco—is on the item itself.

For the physical description, the specific material designation
is *model*. Information on the composition of the materials used
to make the model and its dimensions, in centimeters, are provided.

A summary note indicates that information on the Empire State
Building is located on the side panel of the container. The manufacturer's number is also given in a note.

This item is given a title main entry.

*Puppet (Chapter 10)*

Chapter 10 provides the rules for describing realia, that is,
actual objects. These realia may be artefacts or replicas of artefacts,

Figure 15
**Puppet**

> Abe [Lincoln] [realia]. — [Austin, Texas : Nancy
> Renfro Studios, 1980?].
> 1 hand puppet : cloth, col. ; 40 cm. high.
> I. Lincoln, Abraham, 1809–1865. II. Nancy
> Renfro Studios (Firm).

or naturally occurring items. The only chapter that can be used to describe a puppet is chapter 10.

The chief source of information for the puppet in figure 15 is the tag on the inside of the puppet. Other information is taken from the manufacturer's catalog. The chief source of information says *Abe,* so this is transcribed as the first part of the title and *Lincoln* is added in square brackets for clarification.

The general material designation that seems most appropriate is *realia.*

Publication, distribution, etc., information comes from the publisher's catalog. The date of manufacture is estimated.

For the physical description, the specific material designation is *hand puppet,* and information on the material used to make the item is provided as well as its dimensions, that is, the height of the item.

For access points the puppet is given a title main entry and an added entry may be made for the manufacturer. Optionally, an added entry is made under the heading for Abraham Lincoln according to rule 21.29B, which states that added entries may be made under any heading "if some catalogue users might suppose that the description . . . would be found under that heading."[2] This would be especially important in a divided catalog, where the subject heading for Lincoln would not appear in the author-title section of the catalog.

*Puzzle (Chapter 10)*

Puzzles, like many other three-dimensional materials, pose a problem of which material-specific rules to select. Since there is only one correct way to put a puzzle together, I consider it a game.

The chief source of information for the puzzle in figure 16 is its container.

The general material designation *game* was selected from the list because assembling the puzzle follows a prescribed set of rules and, thus, satisfied the *AACR2* definition of a game.

Figure 16
**Puzzle**

> School of fish [game]. — Phillips-Avon, Maine :
> Lauri, [197–?].
> 1 jigsaw puzzle : rubber, col. ; 28 x 21 cm.
> Lauri: 2122.
> I. Lauri (Firm).

Figure 17
**Realia**

> [1978 United States coins] [realia]. — Denver,
> Colo. : United States Mint, 1978.
> 5 coins, 1 medallion ; in cellophane wrapper,
> 14 x 9 cm.
> Title supplied by cataloger.
> Contents: 1 penny — 1 nickel — 1 dime
> — 1 quarter — 1 half dollar — 1 U.S. Mint me-
> dallion.
> I. United States Mint (Denver, Colo.). II. United
> States. Department of the Treasury. III. Title:
> United States coins (1978).

Publication, distribution, etc., information can be found in the chief source of information, though the date must be supplied by the cataloger.

Physical description consists of the specific material designation *jigsaw puzzle,* with a description of the material from which the item is made.

A note contains the manufacturer's number.

Access points include main entry under title and an added entry for the manufacturer.

*Realia (Chapter 10)*

These souvenir coins from the United States Mint in Denver (figure 17) are considered three-dimensional objects. They were grouped together by the mint.

There is no formal chief source of information because no information is provided on the cellophane container, which acts as the unifying element. Consequently, all information comes from the items themselves.

A title is supplied because the item is composed of multiple parts and lacks a collective title. This is only one option. The cataloger could decide to transcribe the information on each coin, following the rules for items lacking a collective title.

The general material designation is *realia.*

The coins were produced by the U.S. Mint in Denver, therefore publication, distribution, etc., information is transcribed.

The physical description details the number of coins, the fact that there is a medallion, and that it is all in a cellophane container.

A note is provided to indicate that the cataloger supplied the title. A contents note describes the coins in the set.

Access points include main entry under title and added entries for the U.S. Mint, the U.S. Department of the Treasury, and a variant title, *United States coins,* with the year.

### Notes

1.  *Anglo-American Cataloguing Rules,* 2nd ed., ed. Michael Gorman and Paul W. Winkler (Chicago: American Library Association, 1978), 564.

2.  *Anglo-American Cataloguing Rules,* 322.

# ■ Cataloging Microcomputer Software: Using the Newly Revised *AACR2* Chapter 9

by Nancy B. Olson

One must remember that cataloging rules have never before been developed in advance of, or even contemporaneously with, the first appearance of a previously unknown medium of documentary communication. It took almost 150 years after the invention of printing before the bibliographic description of printed books could be said to have received systematic attention; and the title page was in existence for 250 years before its implications for that description, so obvious to us, were embodied in rules or recognized consistently in practice . . . . In our more hurried age, we must risk groping in the dark as the nature, format, internal identification patterns, and use of the various nonbook materials settle and show a greater degree of predictability. Our users need catalog records *now*, not when media manufacturers have finally stabilized the identification of their products.[1]

Hagler's plea, made in 1979 about nonbook materials, has been echoed time after time by those needing rules for cataloging microcomputer software. This plea has been answered by the recent complete revision of chapter 9 of the *Anglo-American Cataloguing Rules*, second edition *(AACR2)*.

Microcomputers were made possible by the invention of the microchip in 1971. Microcomputers began to be used in education about 1977, and the first commercial educational software for them was available about 1978. Soon after, librarians began to inquire how to catalog this software.

The original chapter 9 of *AACR2* contained rules for cataloging

Nancy B. Olson is Professor at Mankato State University (Minn.) where she is an audiovisual cataloger. Recipient of the Esther Piercy Award of the Resources and Technical Services Division of the American Library Association, she is the author of *Cataloging of Audiovisual Materials, Index to the Cataloging Service Bulletin,* and other works.

"machine-readable data files." Microcomputer software fell within the scope of chapter 9 but, because microcomputers and their software were not in existence at the time of the development of the chapter, the rules of chapter 9 did not specifically cover their cataloging, nor did they include provisions for some of the specific needs of microcomputer software users.

Because of these problems with chapter 9, a task force was created by the American Library Association's Resources and Technical Services Division, Cataloging and Classification Section, Committee on Cataloging: Description and Access (CC:DA) and charged with preparation of guidelines for cataloging microcomputer software. The report of the task force was adopted by CC:DA in January 1984, and published as *Guidelines for Using AACR2 Chapter 9 for Cataloging Microcomputer Software.*[2]

CC:DA later studied reaction to these *Guidelines,* and began preparation of proposals for formal revision. Meanwhile, librarians in Canada, the United Kingdom, and Australia were also studying the problems of cataloging microcomputer software.

The Joint Steering Committee for the Revision of the Anglo-American Cataloguing Rules (JSC) is the international body responsible for maintenance of the rules. The British submitted a formal proposal for revision of *AACR2* chapter 9 to JSC late in 1984. During 1985 this proposal was discussed by JSC and by cataloging committees in the participating countries. The Joint Steering Committee directed Michael Gorman, one of the editors of *AACR2,* to prepare a draft revision of chapter 9 for JSC action. Several drafts were prepared during 1985–86 and discussed by cataloging committees in the four countries involved. As a result of action taken in October 1986 at a London meeting of JSC, a provisional version of the new chapter, which was published in spring 1987, contains these new rules.[3] A consolidated version in 1988 will contain revised rules based on this provisional chapter.

### Cataloging Computer Files

*Terminology*
*Computer files* is the term used in the revised chapter 9 for both data files and programs. No distinction is made between files for mainframe computers, minicomputers, or microcomputers.

*Scope*
All types of computer files are included. Both published and unpublished materials are included.

Electronic devices are not covered by chapter 9; the cataloger is referred to chapter 10 to catalog these items.

### Chief Source of Information

The chief source of information is the title screen or screens. If there is no title screen, information from menus, program statements, or other internal evidence is the next choice for chief source of information.

If this information is not available (whether unavailable because the cataloger does not have access to a computer to run the item, or because there is no title screen, menu, etc. when the item is run), information is to be taken (in this order) from:

the physical carrier or its labels
accompanying material
the container
published descriptions
other sources.

This means we are expected, if we have access to a computer, to run the item and use the information from the title screen(s) for cataloging. Some programs have no title screen(s). Other programs do not display the title information until the user has gone through a number of preparatory steps related to the hardware being used (e.g., entering the number of disk drives and their internal locations, name of printer, etc.). With some programs, one must remove the write-protect tab and enter first and last name of the user before the program will proceed to the title information.

### Title and Statement of Responsibility Area

The title and statement of responsibility are to be recorded as directed in *AACR2* chapter 1.

The general material designation for the revised chapter 9 is *computer file*. The term *machine-readable data file* is to be deleted from the GMD lists in rule 1.1C1.

### Edition Area

The words *edition, issue, version, release, level, update* and their equivalents are considered to indicate editions.

One must be careful when cataloging computer files to differentiate between a new version of the software and the version of the operating system needed to run that software. Both are frequently expressed as *version 3.3* or some other decimal number. The term that refers to the operating system may include the letters

*DOS* or *CP/M* or some combination of numbers and letters, including the letters *os* for operating system. A statement referring to the version of the software is recorded as an edition statement; the statement referring to the version of the operating system needed to run that software is included in the *System requirements* note.

### File Characteristics Area

Area 3 is to be used when cataloging computer files. The area is made up of two parts.

The type of file is indicated by one of the following terms:

Computer data
Computer program(s)
Computer data and program(s)

The term *computer* in this area is optional if the GMD is used; the Library of Congress may issue a rule interpretation on this when they begin their CIP project for cataloging microcomputer software.

If the information is readily available, the number of file or files is given, as well as the number of records and/or bytes, the number of program statements and/or bytes, and the combined information for those items including both data and programs.

Computer data (1 file : 225 records)
Computer program (23 statements)
Computer program (1 file : 263 statements)
Computer program (2 files : 400, 500 bytes)

### Publication, Distribution, etc., Area

Information for this area is to be recorded as directed in *AACR2* chapter 1.

### Physical Description Area

This area is not used when cataloging a computer file only available by remote access.

#### EXTENT OF ITEM

The number of physical items is given, with the appropriate term:

computer cartridge
computer cassette

computer disk
computer reel

A more specific term may be used, if desired:

computer chip cartridge
computer tape cartridge
computer tape reel
computer laser optical disk

The word *computer* in the above lists is optional. We await LC rule interpretation on this use.

### OTHER PHYSICAL DETAILS

The terms *sd.* and *col.* are used as needed. Optionally, physical characteristics of disks may be included here. The number of sides used, recording density, and sectoring are included.

### DIMENSIONS

Disks: Measure the diameter in inches, to the next ¼ in.

Cartridges: Measure the edge of the cartridge that is to be inserted into the machine, in inches, to the next ¼ in.

Cassettes: Measure length by width in inches.

### ACCOMPANYING MATERIAL

Information is to be recorded as in *AACR2* chapter 1.

*Series Area*

Information is to be recorded as in *AACR2* chapter 1.

*Notes Area*

Rule 1.7A5 allows us, when appropriate, to combine two or more notes to make one note. Notes are to be used in the order given below.

### NATURE AND SCOPE

To be used unless the information is apparent from the rest of the bibliographic record.

*Example:* An educational game.

### SYSTEM REQUIREMENTS

To be used to specify the make and model of computer on which the item is designed to run, the amount of memory required, the name of the operating system, software requirements including programming language, and kind and characteristics of needed peripherals.

*Example:* System requirements: Macintosh; 512K; LaserWriter.

MODE OF ACCESS
To be used to specify the mode of access if a file is available only by remote access.

LANGUAGE
To be used for language of content, not for programming language.

*Example:* Language of text: German.

SOURCE OF TITLE PROPER
To be used for *all* bibliographic records.

*Examples:*  Title from container.
Title from title screens.
Title from disk label.

VARIATIONS IN TITLE
To be used to note any title appearing on other than the chief source of information that differs significantly from the title proper.

*Example:*  Title on disk label: Genetics.
(*Title proper of above is* Elementary genetics)

PARALLEL TITLES AND OTHER TITLE INFORMATION
To be used for parallel titles and other title information that were not recorded in the title and statement of responsibility area; give only if considered important.

*Example:*  Title on guide: Getting ready to read and add.
(*Title proper:* Préparation à la lecture et à l'addition)

STATEMENTS OF RESPONSIBILITY
To be used to record the information not given in the chief source of information, or not given prominently there, concerning programmers, system designers, etc.

*Examples:* Designed by Nelson G. Hernandez.
Game design, Dan and Bill Bunten ; program, Dan Bunten.
Copyright by Richard Bruce Rickard.

EDITION AND HISTORY
To be used for information about earlier editions.

*Example:* First ed. called: Step by step.
(*Title proper of this example:* New step by step)

FILE CHARACTERISTICS
To be used for file characteristics not included in the file characteristics area.

*Example:* File size varies.

PUBLICATION, PRODUCTION, DISTRIBUTION, ETC.
To be used for any detail not given in the publication, distribution, etc., area, but considered important.

*Example:* "Published in the U.K. for the Schools Council by Longman"—Title page of guide.

PHYSICAL DESCRIPTION
To be used for any important information not given in the physical description area.

*Examples:* One disk contains main dictionary, one the supplementary dictionary.
Second disk is back-up.

ACCOMPANYING MATERIAL
To be used to describe accompanying material not given in the physical description area.

*Example:* Manual: Logo for the Apple II / Harold Abelson and Leigh Klotz. Cambridge, MA : MIT, c1982. — 59 p. ; 24 cm.

SERIES
To be used for any important information not given in the series area.

*Example:* Issued also as part of Tax management series.

DISSERTATIONS
To be used for the standard dissertation note when applicable.

*Example:* Thesis (M.S.)—Mankato State College, 1972.

AUDIENCE
To be used to note the intended audience or intellectual level if the information is given on the item or in its documentation.

*Example:* For use by fourth-grade students.

OTHER FORMATS
To be used to list other formats in which the work is available.

*Example:* Available on disk for Apple II, on cassette for TRS-80.

SUMMARY
To be used for a brief objective summary of the content of the software unless the information is obvious from the rest of the bibliographic description.

*Example:* Summary: Student research teams organize the excavation of a recently discovered historical site in a simulation that requires them to collect data and formulate theories about the origins of the people who once lived there.

CONTENTS
To be used to list the contents of the file, either formally or informally.

*Examples:* Includes 9 versions of the game.
Contents: Crimex — Elect1 — Elect2 — Elect3 — Energy — Limits — Future — Policy — USpop — Cleanup.

NUMBERS BORNE BY THE ITEM
To be used for any numbers on the item if they seem important. The numbers are to be quoted if not preceded by a descriptive word or phrase.

*Example:* "No. 1881."

LOCAL NOTES

To be used for notes that apply only to the copy being cataloged. To provide information of importance to patrons of the library cataloging the item.

*Examples:* On Reserve in the ERC.
Use restricted to Sociology 454 class.

"WITH" NOTES

To be used for a separately titled part of an item lacking a collective title. In the note list the other separately titled parts of the item.

*Example:* With: Letter game—Spelling zoo.

## Access Points

Add an added entry for make and model of computer on which the file is to run under rule 21.29D. In the MARC format, field 753 has been established for this access point.

Some fully cataloged examples follow. Screen displays follow card-formatted entries.

Kinnear, Judith F.
    Catlab [computer file] : a genetics simulation / J.F. Kinnear. — Computer data and program. — Iowa City, Iowa : Conduit, c1982.
    1 computer disk : sd., col. ; 5 1/4 in. + 8 slides (col.) + instructor manual.
    System requirements: Apple II.
    Title from title screen.
    Summary: Teaches principles of genetics through a simulation using cats with different coat patterns and colors.
        I. Conduit.   II. Apple II.   III. Title.

**Figure 1**

                                    **Catlab**
                                    **A Genetics Simulation**

**Title screen**    **J. F. Kinnear**
**information**     **Melbourne State College, Australia**

                    **A CONDUIT Reviewed and Tested Package**
                    **Copyright 1982 by J. F. Kinnear**

**Figure 3**

Corl, Terry.
 Quick-search librarian [computer file] / by Terry Corl & Paul K. Warme. — Version 1.1. — Computer program. — State College, PA : Interactive Microware, c1982.
 1 computer disk ; 5 1/4 in. + instruction manual.
 System requirements: Apple II+ ; 48K or Apple IIe; 64K.
 Title from title screen.
 Summary: Allows user to create a personal data base containing references to journals. References can be entered, edited, searched, sorted, and printed.
 I. Warme, Paul K.  II. Interactive Microware, Inc.  III. Apple II+.  IV. Apple IIe.  V. Title.  VI. Title: Quick search librarian.

Interactive Microware, Inc.
Copyright 1982
Version 1.1

Quick-Search Librarian

By Terry Corl *
Paul K. Warme

**Title screen**

**Figure 2**

Conrad, John R.
 Spelling bee games [computer file]. — Version 1.0. — Computer program. — Agoura, CA : Edu-Ware Services, c1981.
 1 computer disk : sd., col. ; 5 1/4 in. + guide. — (Dragonware)
 System requirements: Apple II; game paddles.
 Title from title screen.
 Copyright and guide by John R. Conrad. Intended audience: Ages 5–10.
 Summary: Word and letter play for early spelling and reading readiness skills.
 Contents: Squadron — Skyhook — Puzzle — Convoy.
 I. Edu-Ware Services.  II. Apple II.  III. Title.  IV. Title: Squadron.  V. Title: Skyhood.  Vi. Title: Puzzle.  VII. Title: Convoy.  VIII. Series.

**SPELLING BEE GAMES**
**Version 1.0**
**c Copyright 1981**
**John R. Conrad**

**Menu screen:**

**(1) Squadron**
**(2) Skyhook**
**(3) Puzzle**
**(4) Convoy**

**Title screen**

MacInTax 1985 [computer file] / developed by Michael W. Morgan with a lot of help from Darlene DuVarney ... [et al]. — Version 1. — Computer data and program. — Camarillo, CA : SoftView, 1986.

1 computer disk ; 3 1/2 in. + 1 manual (41 p. : ill. ; 20 cm.)

System requirements: Macintosh; 512K; printer.

Title from title screen.

Summary: For preparing federal income tax returns; includes all the basic schedules and tables.

I. DuVarney, Darlene.  II. Morgan, Michael W.  III. SoftView, Inc.  IV. Macintosh.  V. Title: MacInTax.

**Figure 5**

Title screen

**MacInTax 1985, Version 1 (Initial Release)**
**Copyright c 1985, 1986 by SoftView, Inc.**
**315 Arneill Road, Suite 215**
**Camarillo, CA 93010**

**Developed by Michael W. Morgan with a log of help from Darlene DuVarney, Tehani Stocks, Richard Hinson, Keith Golden, and Alan Wootton.**

---

dBASE II [computer file]. — Ver 2.41A. — Computer program. — Englewood Cliffs, N.J. : Prentice-Hall, c1984.

1 computer disk ; 5 1/4 in. + 1 workbook (231 p. : ill. ; 24 cm.). — (IBM PC Apprentice. Personal computer learning series)

System requirements: IBM PC; printer.

Title from disk label.

Workbook by Deborah Stone; software copyright by Ashton-Tate.

Summary: Tutorial on use of computer program dBASE II.

I. Stone, Deborah.  II. Prentice-Hall, Inc.  III. Ashton-Tate (Firm).  IV. IBM PC.  V. Series.

**Figure 4**

Title screen

**dBASE II/86    Ver 2.41A    1 June 1984**
**Copyright c Ashton-Tate 1984**
**This is a restricted educational version of dBASE II (TM) from Ashton-Tate as part of the**
**IBM APPRENTICE PROGRAM**
**by Prentice-Hall**

## Subject Analysis

Subject headings are not covered by *AACR2*. An ALA *ad hoc* subcommittee prepared guidelines for subject analysis and classification of microcomputer software. These guidelines, *Guidelines on Subject Access to Microcomputer Software*,[4] recommend catalogers treat software in the same way other materials are treated for subject headings and classification. They specifically caution the user to assign subject headings for the content of the software, rather than for its form. If a form subdivision is desired, the guidelines suggest —*Software* as such a subdivision.

### Notes

1. Ronald Hagler, "Nonbook Materials: Chapters 7 through 11," in *The Making of a Code: The Issues Underlying AACR2* (Chicago: American Library Association, 1980), 73.

2. Committee on Cataloging: Description and Access, Cataloging and Classification Section, Resources and Technical Services Division, American Library Association, *Guidelines for Using AACR2 Chapter 9 for Cataloging Microcomputer Software* (Chicago: American Library Association, 1984).

3. *Anglo-American Cataloguing Rules, Second Edition, Chapter 9: Computer Files Draft Revision* (Chicago: American Library Association, 1987).

4. Ad Hoc Subcommittee on Subject Access to Microcomputer Software, Subject Analysis Committee, Cataloging and Classification Section, Resources and Technical Services Division, American Library Association, *Guidelines on Subject Access to Microcomputer Software* (Chicago: American Library Association, 1986).

■

■ MARC Tagging for Nonbook
Materials

by Sheila S. Intner

The first MARC (MAchine-Readable Cataloging) format was designed for computer communication of bibliographic information
for books by the Library of Congress (LC). Afterward, when the
need became obvious, formats for other kinds of materials were
devised, beginning with serials, which presented coding problems
different from books. Later, MARC formats were designed to accommodate cataloging for other physical manifestations of intellectual or artistic works. Formats now exist for films and other
visual materials, computer files, manuscripts, maps, music, and
sound recordings. Formats for these nonbook material groups were
added at different times.

The process of establishing and revising the MARC formats is
a continuing one shared by the MARC Development Office at LC,
the four bibliographic utilities, that is, OCLC (Online Computer
Library Center), RLIN (Research Libraries Information Network),
UTLAS (University of Toronto Libraries Automated System), and
WLN (Western Library Network, formerly Washington Library Network), and an interdivisional committee of the American Library
Association called the Committee on Representation in Machine-
Readable Form of Bibliographic Information (MARBI). It is similar
to the revision process for the cataloging code (AACR2), in which
several groups participate. Designing or altering the MARC formats
is not only a matter of making rules, basically the prerogative of
LC, but also interpreting and applying them, the responsibility of
the bibliographic utilities, as well as policy making for all U.S.
users of the MARC formats, which is the emphasis of MARBI.

Each different material group has features in common with
books, features that are analogous, but not identical to books, and
features that are distinctive, though not necessarily unique. The
MARC formats for nonbook materials include some fields identical
to those in the Books Format; some fields with the same interpretation for the field as a whole, but specific codes for particular

medium groups; and some fields that only have meaning for the nonbook items in a specific material group. Part of the difficulty of encoding bibliographic records for nonbook materials is learning these new fields, the new versions of old fields, and distinguishing them from old, familiar fields used in the same way as they are for books.

The MFBD—MARC Formats for Bibliographic Data—are arranged in one sequence from the first field (001) to the last (9xx) without regard to any particular format. Along with an explanation of each field in the format and the codes and/or data that can be recorded in it is a list of formats with checks under those for which the field or subfield is relevant. In contrast, OCLC has a different publication for each format in which only the fields and data relevant to the format are included. OCLC's documentation is much easier to follow and to use. Other bibliographic utilities have their own documentation, and it is best for catalogers to learn to use whichever is appropriate for their institution.

There are other differences among the LC version of MARC and those used in the bibliographic utilities. Some utilities have added fields, some have added formats, and some have translated fields from one kind of coding to another. Examples from the OCLC bibliographic network explain these variations from the MFBD: The 049 field (Local Holdings) in the Audiovisual Format is an example of a field defined within the OCLC network and used by its participants; the Sound Recordings Format is an example of a separate format defined for local participants; and the initial alphabetic abbreviations containing codes describing the work being cataloged which appear on screen before the 010 field are really a translation of the MFBD's 008 field in a different layout. RLIN has done the same thing for both the 007 and 008 fields. The changes to the fixed fields were instituted to make this coded information easier for staff to enter and to understand. The important thing to realize is that each utility and even each institution within a single utility is going to exercise local options or interpret encoding rules differently. Far from being deleterious, this is desirable in a pluralistic environment, provided individuality is not stretched beyond the limits of standard practice, and the resulting data is not unsharable.

## General Information about the MARC Formats

Data in the MARC formats may be transcribed into fixed or variable fields. In the former, information is coded into a fixed number of characters and entered in a fixed form, hence the name *fixed field*. In the latter, although the sequence of data elements in a field is prescribed (e.g., for personal name main entries, names, qualifying phrases, and dates are entered in that order), the content—the words or numbers—in each element, and therefore the field as a whole, may vary in length and form. Personal authors may have first, middle, and last names or they may be known by a single name (e.g., Homer); titles may have one word or many or may be divided into a main title and subtitle; editions may be called *2nd*, *revised and enlarged*, or *version 2.0*. Thus, the fields in which this varying data is represented are called *variable fields*. Differences among the formats occur in both fixed and variable fields.

Just as *AACR2's* chapters for choice and form of entries apply to all materials, all MARC formats have the same tags or content designators for main entries, added entries, subjects, uniform titles, titles proper, edition statements, material specific data, publication, distribution information, physical descriptions, series statements, and most of the notes. The ISBN or ISSN and terms of availability are also the same for all formats. Proposals to integrate the various formats completely have been put forward and, as of this writing, discussions about it continue.

In the following paragraphs, coding and tagging according to the OCLC version of MARC are shown for examples of the audiovisual media, scores, sound recordings, maps, and computer files, as of this writing still known as machine-readable data files. (Author's note: OCLC–MARC was selected because it is currently in use for cataloging in more libraries than any other subset of MARC and because the documentation furnished by the utility is complete, well-illustrated, and easy to understand by noninitiates. In no way is the use of OCLC–MARC intended to create a bias toward that utility based on any other factors.)

### Special Fields in the Audiovisual Format

The Audiovisual Format, which began life as LC's Films Format and has just been transformed into the Visual Materials Format, although OCLC will retain the use of Audiovisual Format, covers a great many individual material forms, making it one of the most complex of the formats. There are, at the moment, four groups of materials covered in it: (1) projected media, such as films, filmstrips, and videorecordings; (2) two-dimensional nonprojected graphic representations, including a variety of opaque, visual items such as flashcards, posters, pictures, photographs, wall-

Figure 1
**Tagging for a videorecording using the Audiovisual Format**

| | | | | | |
|---|---|---|---|---|---|
| Type: g | Bib lvl: m | Govt pub: | Lang: eng | Source: d | Leng: 98 |
| | Enc lvl: I | Type mat: | Ctry: cau | Dat tp: s | MEBE: 0 |
| Tech: 1 | Mod rec: | Accomp mat: | | | |
| Desc: a | Int lvl: g | Dates: 1971, | | | |

1 040      xxx $c xxx

2 007      v $b f $c    $d c $e n $f a $g h $h o

3 245 04    The Anderson tapes : $h videorecording / $c produced by Robert M. Weitman ; directed by Sidney Lumet ; screenplay by Frank R. Pierson.

4 260      [Burbank, Calif.] : $b Columbia Pictures Home Entertainment, $c c1971.

5 300      1 videocassette (98 min.) : $b sd., col. ; $c 1/2 in.

6 500      Title from label.

7 500      Based on the novel by Lawrence Sanders.

8 511      Sean Connery, Dyan Cannon, Martin Balsam, Alan King.

9 508      Music by Quincy Jones.

10 500      VHS format.

11 520      An ex-convict plots the robbery of an entire apartment building while the authorities monitor his movements with electronic devices.

12 700 10    Weitman, Robert M.

13 700 10    Lumet, Sidney.

14 700 10    Pierson, Frank R.

15 700 10    Sanders, Lawrence. $t Anderson tapes.

16 700 10    Connery, Sean.

17 700 10    Cannon, Dyan.

18 700 10    Balsam, Martin.

19 700 10    King, Alan.

charts, etc.; (3) three-dimensional artefacts and realia (not yet implemented); and (4) kits. Figures 1, 2 and 3 show how the three different types of entries currently available in the OCLC database look. (Remember: Mnemonic fixed fields at the top of each entry represent the coding of features of the item's physical and intellectual content contained in the MFBD's 008 field.) There is no figure for the fourth group because as of this writing the format has not yet been implemented.

### Coding and Tagging

Type: g/k/o/r   This choice defines the four groups of materials coded in this format: g = projected audiovisual media, now includes filmstrips, slides, and transparencies in ad-

Figure 2
**Tagging for flashcards using the Audiovisual Format**

Type: k   Bib lvl: m   Govt pub:        Lang: eng   Source: d   Leng:
          Enc lvl: I   Type mat: o       Ctry: cau   Dat tp: s   MEBE: s
Tech: n   Mod rec:     Accomp mat:
Desc: a   Int lvl: b   Dates: 1974,

1 040      xxx $c xxx
2 007      k $b o $c    $d b $e c $f
3 100 10   Fenderson, Julia K.
4 245 14   The reading box $h flashcard : $b 150 reading games &
activities / $c Julia K. Fenderson.
5 250      Rev. ed.
6 260      Carson, Calif. : $b Educational Insights, $c 1974.
7 300      154 cards : $b b&w ; $c 10 x 15 cm. in box.
8 520      "This Reading Box is intended as a source of a
variety of supplementary aids, ideas and techniques for your
reading programs."
9 505 0    Reading readiness — Listening skill builders —
Vocabulary builders — Phonics — Choral verse — Reading
through writing — Comprehension skills — Dramatic play —
Dictionary and reference skills — Speed reading — Book reports — Continuum of reading skills.
10 500     Educational Insights: 9112.

Figure 3
**Tagging for a kit using the Audiovisual Format**

Type: o   Bib lvl: m   Govt pub:        Lang: eng   Source: d   Leng:
          Enc lvl: I   Type mat: b       Ctry: nyu   Dat tp: s   MEBE: 0
Tech: n   Mod rec:     Accomp mat:
Desc: a   Int lvl:     Dates: 1973,

1 040      xxx $c xxx
2 007      g $b o $c    $d c $e j $f b $g f $h f
3 245 00   Recycling $h kit : $b an ecology study / $c presented
by the Aluminum Association.
4 260 0    New York : $b the Association, $c [1973?].
5 300      1 filmstrip (78 fr.) : $b col. ; $c 35 mm. in container, 31 x 32 x 6 cm. + $e 1 cassette (ca. 30 min.) + 1
teacher's guide + 1 booklet (45 p.).
6 500      Booklet lists recycling centers.
7 500      Cassette with audible and inaudible signals.
8 710 20   Aluminum Association (United States).

dition to motion pictures and videorecordings which were formerly the only media given this code and called *principal audiovisual media;* k = pictures, designs, and other two-dimensional nonprojectible graphics; o = kits; and r = three-dimensional materials, that is, artefacts and realia. Correct coding of this subfield is extremely important, since other parts of the record hinge on which type of item is being described. The format is still being altered to accommodate 3-dimensional materials, and updates to existing formats will continue to be made.

007     Details the physical attributes of the item being described. Begins with the specific material designation and includes much more information than provided in uncoded form in the 300 field. Books Format includes 007 for the coding of microforms. LC alone creates a single master record for all manifestations of a work (i.e., an item put out as an 8mm or 16mm motion picture and ½ inch VHS or Beta video, etc.) with multiple 007s for each subformat available; all other cataloging agencies should create a separate record for each physical manifestation it has in hand.

033     Code the place and date of recording (i.e., filming, taping, etc.) in this field if the data is available in the cataloging record and is important to the cataloging agency.

245 $c and 260 $c     Problems here are concerned with *who* is entered for statement of responsibility (245) and publication, distribution statement (260). They are not coding, but cataloging problems. An LC rule interpretation gives the principle for statement of responsibility as persons/bodies with overall responsibility for the item rather than only for one aspect (e.g., the producer or director rather than the composer of the music). Performers are not listed in 245 unless their contribution goes beyond mere performance of their role, as Clint Eastwood might be named for some of the films he conceived, directed, wrote, etc. In 260, the persons/bodies releasing and/or distributing the item should be named, not the producer of the item (who should be named in 245) responsible for the intellectual or technical content of the item. (See the earlier chapter on "Cataloging Motion Pictures and Videorecordings Using *AACR2* Chapter 7.")

508/511     Cast and credits notes are important in cataloging motion pictures and videorecordings. Only principals in the cast and technical production should be included, not an entire cast of characters or all assistants, associates, or other subordinates. Proper coding of the indicators will produce system-supplied print constants appropriate for each of these two fields.

500    A physical description note (7.7B10) is necessary to give additional information about the physical format of a motion picture or video. In particular, it is the appropriate place to identify the particular type of videocassette to which an item belongs, that is, to distinguish between VHS and Beta formats, since the 300 field does not contain information in eye-readable form that does this.

520    Summary notes are important for motion pictures and videos, particularly because these media are not likely to be easily browsed. This lack is due to their location on closed stacks or the unavailability of hardware for playback, or both. The result is that clients frequently must select motion pictures and videos from their catalog descriptions alone. This is much easier if an objective summary is included in the entry.

## Special Fields in the Scores Format

Comp    This mnemonic stands for *form of composition* and consists of a two-character code selected from a list of alternatives based on *LCSH*. If a score contains more than one type of composition, *mu* for multiple is entered here and the individual codes are entered in the companion field, 047.

Format  A one-character code is entered here to identify the type of score being cataloged, such as full score, accompaniment for keyboard, voice miniature or study size score, etc.

Prts    The presence or absence of parts is given in a one-character code.

028     The publisher's and/or plate number is entered here and the selection of appropriate indicators enable it to print as the first note and/or as an added entry. If notes and/or entries are not desired, those options are also available.

047     This field should be used only when the fixed field Comp is *mu*. Then the various codes (the same list as in the Comp field) are entered here in a series of $a's.

048    Information about the number of instruments in ensembles or voices (with or without accompaniment) is given here in coded form. Certain types of compositions are not included, however, such as operas.

098 16    If you use the Dickinson Decimal Classification of Musical Compositions, this is the correct tag and these are the correct indicators to be used for the class number.

240    Since many musical compositions require uniform titles (according to AACR2), this field is included here. Four possible options for the indicators permit or suppress printing on cards and the creation of added entries. The following list of subfields includes a selection of elements frequently used in uniform titles for scores: $k = form subheading, for example, *Selections*; $n = number, such as a serial number (Symphonies, *no. 5*), opus or thematic catalog number, or a date used as a number; $s = version, for example, Messiah. *Vocal score.*; $m = medium of performance; $o = arrangement statement, abbreviated *arr.*; $r = key signature. (Note: This list is not exhaustive.)

## Special Fields in the Sound Recordings Format

The Sound Recordings Format is divided into two groups of materials: musical and nonmusical (also called *spoken*) sound recordings, depending on the content of the recording. Coding the two kinds of items is very similar, although several of the fields listed below are identified as belonging to only one of them. See figure 4 for an example of the use of this format.

Type: i/j    Identifies the group of sound recordings to which the item belongs: i = nonmusical; j = musical.

Comp:    A two-letter code that identifies the type of musical composition on a musical sound recording. A long list of composition types and codes are provided. Nonmusical recordings are coded *nn*.

007    As in the Audiovisual Format, this field is a coded version of the 300, with additional attributes of the physical medium included. Here is a case where the format defines the data encoded in the field. Within this format, unlike the Audiovisual Format where each type of material has a different set of values for this field, both types of recordings are treated alike. Differences in coding occur depending on the storage medium of the recording, such as disc; cassette, cartridge, or reel-to-reel tape; etc.

Figure 4
**Tagging for a musical sound recording using the Sound Recordings Format**

| Type: j | Bib lvl: m | Lang: N/A | Source: d | Accomp mat: |
|---------|-----------|-----------|-----------|-------------|
|         | Mod rec:  | Comp: pp  | Format: n | Parts: n    |
| Repr:   | Enc lvl: I | Ctry: cau | Dat tp: s | MEBE: 1     |
| Desc: a | Int lvl:  | LTxt:     | Dates: 1968, |          |

| | | |
|---|---|---|
| 1 | 040 | xxx $c xxx |
| 2 | 007 | s $b d $d b $e s $f m $g e $h n $i n |
| 3 | 028 01 | ST-2895 $b Capitol |
| 4 | 110 20 | Beach Boys (Musical group). |
| 5 | 245 10 | Friends $h sound recording / $c The Beach Boys. |
| 6 | 260 0 | Hollywood, Calif. : $b Capitol Records, $c [1968?]. |
| 7 | 300 | 1 sound disc (26 min.) : $b analog, 33 1/3 rpm, stereo. ; $c 12 in. |
| 8 | 500 | Songs. |
| 9 | 505 0 | Meant for you / B. Wilson ; M. Love (:38) — Friends / B. Wilson ; D. Wilson ; C. Wilson ; A. Jardine (2:32) — Wake the world / B. Wilson ; A. Jardine (1:29) — Be here in the mornin' / B. Wilson ; D. Wilson ; M. Love (2:17) — When a man needs a woman / B. Wilson; D. Wilson ; A. Jardine ; S. Korthof ; J. Parks (2:07) — Passing by / B. Wilson (2:24) — Anna Lee, the healer / M. Love ; B. Wilson (1:51) — Little bird ; Be still / D. Wilson ; S. Kalinich (2:02 ; 1:24) — Busy doin' nothin' / B. Wilson (3:05) — Diamond Head / A. Vescozo ; L. Ritz ; J. Ackley ; B. Wilson (3:39) — Transcendental meditation / B. Wilson ; M. Love ; A. Jardine (1:51). |

028     Manufacturer's label and number. Similar to the publisher's number in the Scores Format. The number is entered in subfield a, label in subfield b. Indicators are coded to generate the first note for this information.

033     As in the Audiovisual Format this field contains information about the recording date and/or place if that information is available in the record and important to the cataloging agency.

511     Cast/Performer: If the recording is nonmusical (Type i), the print constant *Cast:* is generated, since narrators, speakers, etc., are considered cast rather than performers. If the recording is musical (Type j), no print constant is supplied and principal performers are listed here. In this format, performers' names are given first, followed by the medium of performance, for example, Itzhak Perlman, violin. This is exactly opposite to the way credits are given for motion

pictures and videorecordings, for example, music, Dmitri Tiomkin.

518     Related to control field 033, information on the place and date of the recording session is entered here.

520     Contents note. Many sound recordings are collections of musical or spoken pieces, sometimes also with different composers/authors and performers. A contents note is necessary to provide, at a minimum, indirect access to these individual works. If a decision is made to provide direct access by means of analytic entries, then this note furnishes the basis on which they may be made.

## Special Fields in the Maps Format

The Maps Format contains a number of the special fields from the serials format that enables catalogers to describe a map serial, for example, a field to enter the frequency of publication, etc. Only some of these are singled out for description. Catalogers have been lobbying for the addition of these fields to other nonbook formats so they would not have to choose between a format appropriate to the physical form of the material or a format appropriate to its publication pattern. See figure 5 for an example of the use of this format.

Base     This fixed field contains a two-character code for the projection of the map in the first two positions and a one-character code for the prime meridian, if specified on the map, in the third position. If no prime meridian is specified, this position is left blank.

Form     Alphabetic codes identifying special format characteristics of the item being cataloged are entered here, for example, d = film negative; e = manuscript; g = relief model; etc.

RecG     This field contains a single character code for the record group to which the item being cataloged belongs, for example, a = single map; b = map series; c = map serial; d = globe.

Relief     Alphabetic codes defining relief types are given here, and up to four different types may be entered for maps displaying more than one type.

034     This control field is used for a coded version of the mathematical data (area 3 in *AACR2*)—scale, projection, and co-ordinates. It is a companion field to the 255, in which this same information appears in eye-readable form. When machine-searching is done by coordinates, it is this strictly for-

Figure 5
**Tagging for a map using the Maps Format**

| Type: e | Bib lvl: m | Lang: eng | Source: d | Form: | Relief: |
|---------|-----------|-----------|-----------|-------|---------|
| RecG: a | Enc lvl: I | Ctry: ohu | Dat tp: s | Govt pub: | Indx: 0 |
| Desc: a | Mod rec: | Base: ^^ | Dates: 1979, | | |

```
 1 040      xxx $c xxx
 2 034  1   a $b 9000000
 3 052      3701 $b N35
 4 110  2   GEO*graphics (Cincinnati, Ohio)
 5 245 10   Nuclear power reactors and prevailing wind patterns
in the continental U.S.A.
 6 255      Scale [ca. 1:9,000,000].
 7 260  0   Cincinnati, Ohio : $b GEO*graphics, $c c1979.
 8 300      1 map : $b col. ; $c 42 x 56 cm., folded to 23 x 29
cm.
 9 500      "Prevailing wind direction based on United States
Department of Commerce data."
10 500      Text and descriptive list of "Commercial nuclear
power reactors in the United States" on verso.
11 650  0   Atomic power-plants $z United States $x Maps.
12 650  0   Winds $z United States $x Maps.
```

matted data that is searchable since it always appears in standard, uniform form.

255    Required by *AACR2* and ISBD(CM), this field contains data for the scale, projection, and coordinates, given in verbal form.

265    The source of acquisition information given in this field is important in shared databases, since there is no reference tool for maps similar to *Books in Print*. LC practice is to include the address of the publisher if it is available.

315    The frequency of a serial map is entered here.

362    Numeric and/or chronological, alphabetical, or other information relating to the sequencing system for serial maps is entered here.

## Special Fields in the Machine-Readable Data Files Format

Like the Maps Format, the Machine-Readable Data Files Format (MRDF)* also contains a number of special fields for serials. All

*As of this writing, a change to "computer files" has not yet been effected.

Figure 6
**Tagging for microcomputer software using the MRDF Format**

Type: m  Bib lvl: m  Govt pub:    Lang: N/A  Source: d  Frequen: n
File: b    Enc lvl: I    Machine: a  Ctry: cau   Dat tp: c   Regulr:
Desc: a    Mod rec:     Dates: 1982, 1980

  1 040       xxx $c xxx

  2 245 00    Stoneware's DB master $h machine-readable data file

  3 250       Ver. 3.02.

  4 260       San Rafael, CA : $b Stoneware, $c 1982, c1980.

  5 300       1 program file on 2 identical computer disks ; $c 5
1/4 in. + $e manual.

  6 500       Data base management program.

  7 500       Title on manual: D B master.

  8 538       System requirements: Apple II, II+, or IIe; 48K; DOS
3.3; two disk drives, printer.

  9 650 0     Data base management.

10 710 20    Stoneware, Inc.

11 740 01    DB master $h machine-readable data file

12 740 01    D B master $h machine-readable data file

the serials fields from the Maps Format are also part of this format, though their descriptions are not repeated below. See figure 6 for an example of the use of this format.

Lang       This field is filled only when the file being cataloged is a text file. The language code appropriate to the language of the text is included here. The field is not intended to record the programming language for program files.

Machine  Only two codes are applicable to this field: a = computer-readable and z = other. The brand (Apple, IBM) of computer or size of computer (mainframe, minicomputer, or microcomputer) is not codable here.

211/214  Computer files often have acronyms or abbreviated versions of the titles appearing in the 245 field; or, if given shorter titles in the 245, there may be longer versions. Field 211 is used for an acronym or shortened title, while 214 is used for a lengthened or augmented title.

516       Information about the general character of the file, for example, computer programs, numeric or text files may be given here as well as more specific information about it, such as its form or the genre of a text file.

538       Technical details about the file are entered in this note as

well as information about system requirements, disk characteristics, and the other systems on which the file can run.
Although there are no print constants for this field, the
Guidelines for Using AACR2 Chapter 9 for Cataloging Microcomputer Software indicate three prefixes for formal
notes when cataloging these materials: System requirements:, Disk characteristics:, and Also runs on:.

556    Information about the documentation accompanying computer files is given here if it explains the contents and use
of the file. The scope note for the field says that information
about materials based on the use, study, or analysis of a
file should be entered in the publications note (field 581).

565    Called the Case file characteristics note, it is used by catalogers for the number of cases or variables making up the
file.

582    Information about related machine-readable files should be
given in this note.

753    This field, which generated much controversy because it
does not conform to AACR2, contains information about the
make and model of the machine on which a file is run ($a),
its programming language ($b), and the operating system it
uses ($c). Access to these elements of the description is im-
portant to users of MRDFs, and they print both as a heading
and as a roman numeraled added entry.

## Conclusion

OCLC and other networks have devised these encoding conventions to enable bibliographic data to be communicated in machine-
readable form, not to help catalogers prepare bibliographic entries.
This point should always be kept in mind when coding and tagging, which can only be done after cataloging is completed. Bibliographic descriptions and main and added entries must be done
according to AACR2. Although there are local fields included in
the formats to accommodate locally devised classification numbers and subject headings, the MARC formats give preference to
the standard tools such as LC, Dewey Decimal, and NLM classi-
fications; and LCSH, Sears List of Subject Headings, NLM Medical
Subject Headings, etc. Catalogers using online data for copy cataloging may have to edit the records they find for local practices
regarding call numbers, but should, in theory at least, be able to

accept the descriptive and subject cataloging as they find it in the databases. Contributing cataloging to a national network carries the responsibility to follow standards as closely and as fully as possible because the cataloging is intended for more than one's own institution.

# ☐ Index

Prepared by Kristina Masiulis